AGRO-ECOLOGICAL LAND RESOURCES ASSESSMENT

FOR AGRICULTURAL DEVELOPMENT PLANNING

A CASE STUDY OF KENYA

RESOURCES DATA BASE AND LAND PRODUCTIVITY

Technical Annex 5

Livestock productivity

A.H. Kassam, H.T. van Velthuizen, P.H. Sloane,
G.W. Fischer and M.M. Shah

Land and Water Development Division
Food and Agriculture Organization of the United Nations
and
International Institute for Applied Systems Analysis
Rome, 1991

Any part of this livestock productivity model and the model parameters therein may be modified in the light of new knowledge and/or new objectives. The model is part of a larger district and national level planning tool, and is expected to be expanded and refined with use.

The designations employed and the presentation of the material in this document do not imply the expression of any opinion whatsoever on the part of FAO or IIASA concerning the legal or constitutional status of any sea area or concerning the delineation of frontiers.

M-51
ISBN 92-5-103389-7

Contents

Figures

Tables

Page

APPENDIX

Page

REPORT AND TECHNICAL ANNEXES

This work is recorded in a main report and technical annexes.

Main Report:
> Agro-ecological Land Resources Assessment for Agricultural Development Planning — A Case Study of Kenya

> Resources Data Base and Land Productivity

Technical annexes:

1   Land Resources

2   Soil Erosion and Productivity

3   Agro-climatic and Agro-edaphic Suitabilities for Barley, Oat, Cowpea, Green gram and Pigeonpea

4   Crop Productivity

5   Livestock Productivity

6   Fuelwood Productivity

7   Systems Documentation Guide to Computer Programs for Land Productivity Assessments

8   Crop Productivity Assessment: Results at District Level

Chapter 1

Introduction

The 'Agro-ecological Land Resources Assessment for Agricultural Development Planning' is a study concerned with the development and implementation of a national level methodology for determination of land use potentials of land resources of individual districts for policy formulation and development planning. This Kenya case study has been carried out by FAO and IIASA in collaboration with the Government of Kenya (FAO 1984).

The work is described in a main report entitled: Resources Data Base and Land Productivity. This report is supported by technical annexes which deal with the details.

This technical annex deals with the livestock productivity model. The climate and soil resources inventories on which the model operates are described in Technical Annex 1.

FIGURE 2.1
Schematic presentation of the livestock productivity model

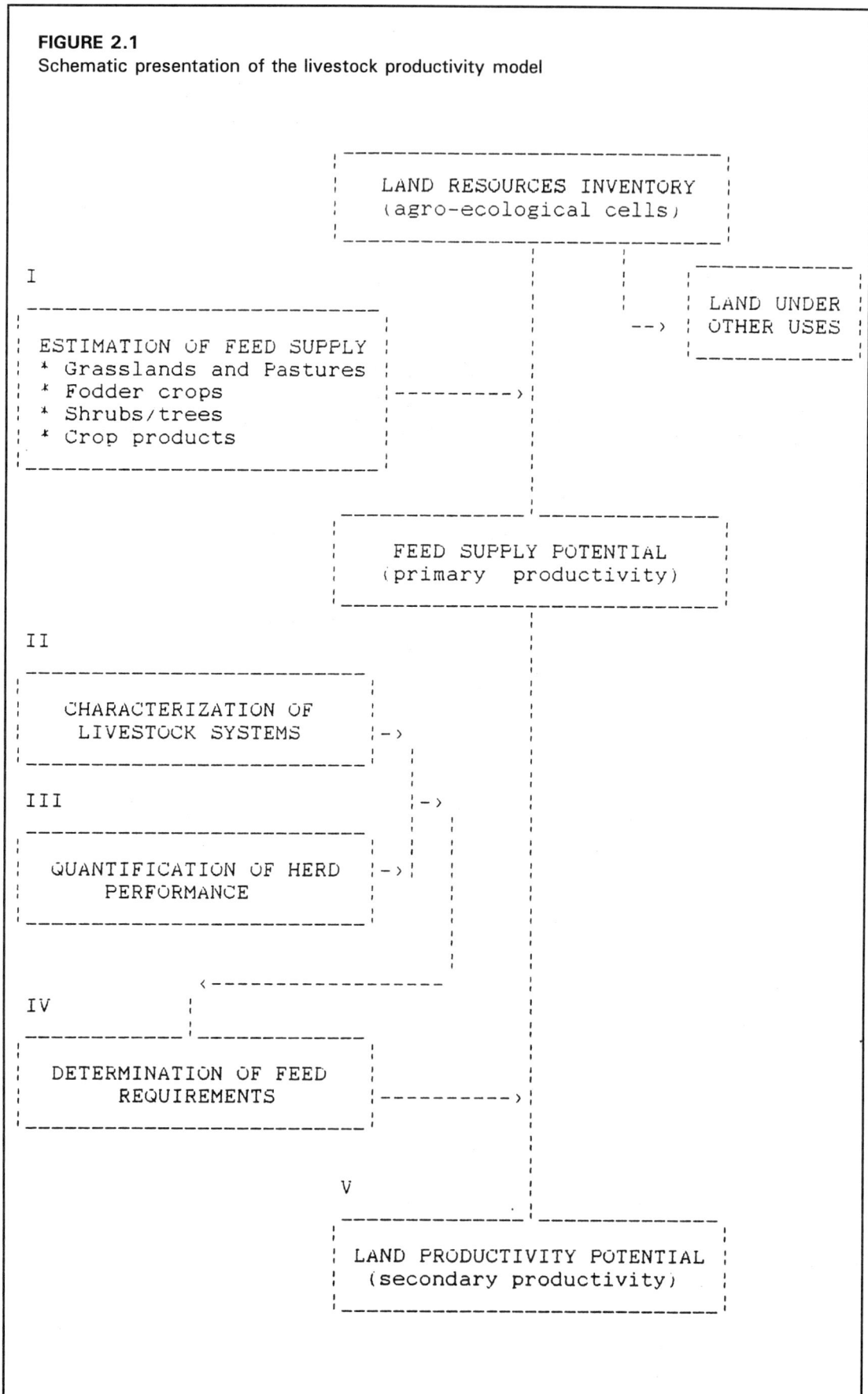

```
                                    ------------------------------
                                    : LAND RESOURCES INVENTORY   :
                                    : (agro-ecological cells)    :
                                    ------------------------------
                                                   :          :
   I                                               :          :        ------------
   ------------------------------                  :          :        : LAND UNDER :
   : ESTIMATION OF FEED SUPPLY  :                  :          :  --> : OTHER USES :
   : * Grasslands and Pastures  :                  :          :        ------------
   : * Fodder crops             : --------->:       :
   : * Shrubs/trees             :                  :
   : * Crop products            :                  :
   ------------------------------                   :
                                                    :
                             ----------------------------------
                             : FEED SUPPLY POTENTIAL          :
                             : (primary productivity)         :
                             ----------------------------------
                                                    :
   II                                               :
   ------------------------------                   :
   : CHARACTERIZATION OF        :                   :
   : LIVESTOCK SYSTEMS          : ->               :
   ------------------------------    :              :
   III                               :->            :
   ------------------------------    :              :
   : QUANTIFICATION OF HERD     : ->:               :
   : PERFORMANCE                :                   :
   ------------------------------                   :
                                                    :
               <------------------                  :
   IV          :                                    :
   ------------------------------                   :
   : DETERMINATION OF FEED      :                   :
   : REQUIREMENTS               : --------->:       :
   ------------------------------                   :
                                                    :
                       V                            :
                             ----------------------------------
                             : LAND PRODUCTIVITY POTENTIAL    :
                             : (secondary productivity)       :
                             ----------------------------------
```

Chapter 2

Methodology

The livestock productivity model is schematically shown in Figure 2.1. It has been conceptualized and applied within the framework of land evaluation guidelines (FAO 1976, 1988a), and follows the FAO Agro-ecological Zones (FAO-AEZ) approach to quantifying land resources and assessing land use potentials (FAO 1978-81; Blair Rains and Kassam 1980).

The livestock productivity model has five parts, namely:

(i)   Estimation of feed supply potential (primary productivity).

(ii) Characterization of livestock systems.

(iii) Determination of herd performance.

(iv) Estimation of feed requirements.

(v)   Quantification of livestock productivity potential (secondary productivity).

The model operates on the land resources inventory described in Technical Annex 1. The five parts of the model, and outline of the land resources inventory are described in the following sections.

FIGURE 3.1
Make-up of land resources data base

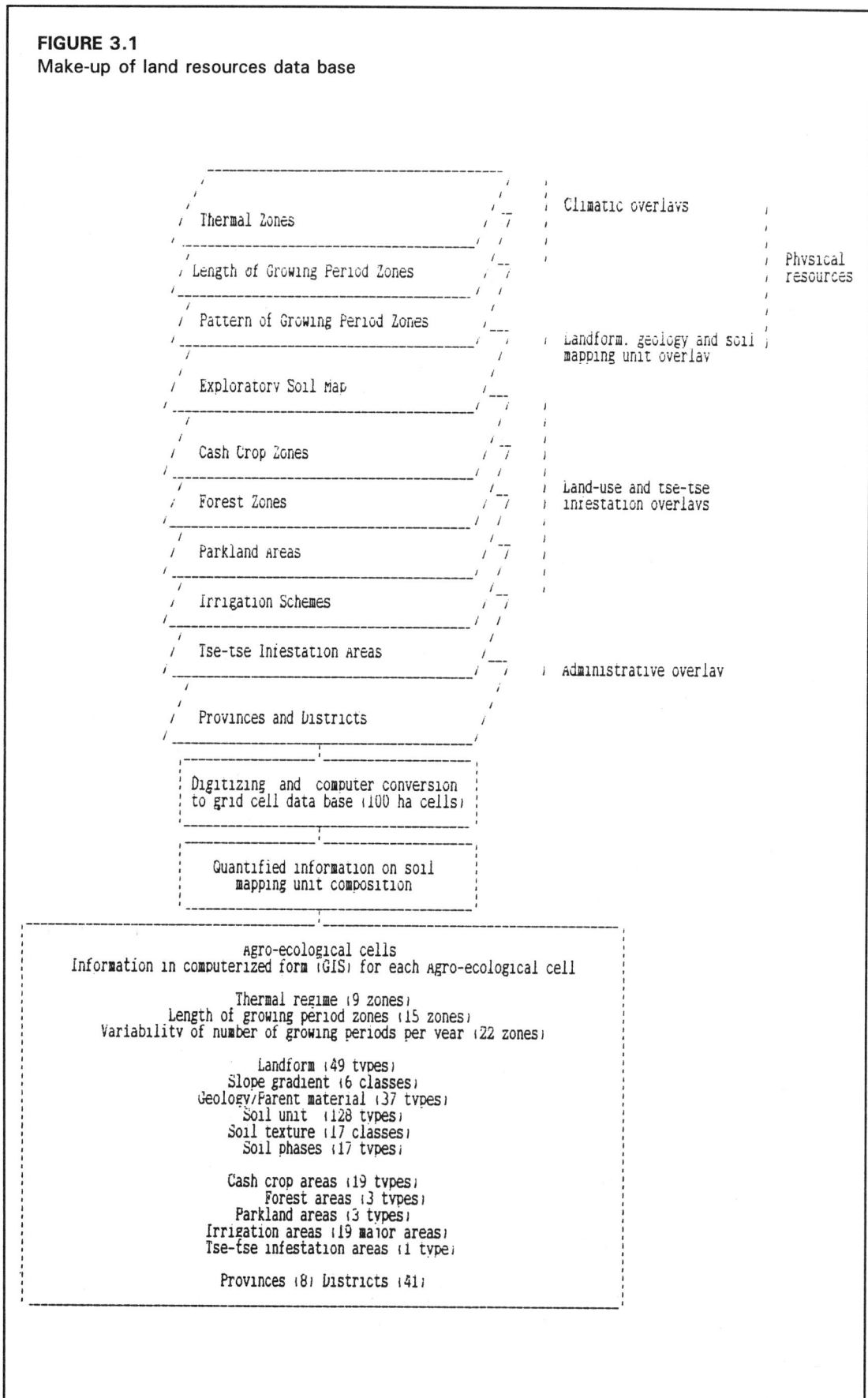

Thermal Zones

Length of Growing Period Zones

Pattern of Growing Period Zones

Exploratory Soil Map

Cash Crop Zones

Forest Zones

Parkland Areas

Irrigation Schemes

Tse-tse Infestation Areas

Provinces and Districts

Climatic overlays

Physical resources

Landform. geology and soil mapping unit overlay

Land-use and tse-tse infestation overlays

Administrative overlay

Digitizing and computer conversion to grid cell data base (100 ha cells)

Quantified information on soil mapping unit composition

Agro-ecological cells
Information in computerized form (GIS) for each Agro-ecological cell

Thermal regime (9 zones)
Length of growing period zones (15 zones)
Variability of number of growing periods per year (22 zones)

Landform (49 types)
Slope gradient (6 classes)
Geology/Parent material (37 types)
Soil unit (128 types)
Soil texture (17 classes)
Soil phases (17 types)

Cash crop areas (19 types)
Forest areas (3 types)
Parkland areas (3 types)
Irrigation areas (19 major areas)
Tse-tse infestation areas (1 type)

Provinces (8) Districts (41)

Chapter 3

Land resources

The land resources data base contains several layers of information on physical resources which allows the creation of unique ecological land units (agro-ecological cells) within which soil, landform and climatic conditions are quantified. This information, compiled at the national level by province and district, constitutes the inventory of the physical land resources.

The climatic resources part consist of three separate thematic layers: the thermal zones layer, the length of growing period zones layer and pattern of number of length of growing period zones layer. The climatic resources inventory is described in Section 4.2.2.

The soil resources layer includes information on soils, landform and geology/parent materials. The soil resources inventory is described in Section 4.2.5.

Additional layers on land uses and administrative subdivisions have also been added. These layers contain inventories of cash crop zones, forest zones, parkland areas, irrigated areas, tse-tse infestation areas and province and district boundaries.

The individual layers have been digitized. The digitized information derived from the individual layers has been converted into a data base of 576,072 grid cells. Each grid cell (one millimeter square) corresponds to 100 ha.

Subsequent to digitizing, the soil map unit composition of each mapping unit and the associated edaphic conditions have been incorporated.

The make-up of the national land resources data base is schematically presented in Figure 3.1. The computerized land resources data base for Kenya records total extents of 90 000 agro-ecological cells. Each cell contains information on:

- Sequence number (NUM)
- Province (PRV)
- District (DIST)
- Thermal Zone (TZ)
- Length of Growing Period Zone (LGP)
- Pattern of Length of Growing Period Zone (PAT)
- Soil Mapping Unit (MPU)
- Landform (LNDFM)
- Geology/Parent Material (GEO)
- Soil Unit (SOIL)

- Soil Texture (TXT)
- Soil Phases (PHASES)
- Cash Crop Zone (CROP)
- Forest Zone (FOR)
- Irrigation Scheme (IRR)
- Tse-tse Infestation Areas (TSE)
- Parkland Area (PARK)
- Extent in hectares (EXTENT).

The land resources data base is available in the form of a grid based geographic information system (GIS). For details, reference should be made to Technical Annex 7.

Chapter 4

Estimation of feed supply

Animals require an uninterrupted and adequate supply of nutritively satisfactory feed. Part I of the livestock productivity model (Figure 2.1) deals with the estimation of feed supply from different sources. A wide variety of plant biomass is eaten by domestic herbivores. The important sources of feed biomass are the grasses, a small number of herbaceous legumes, leaves and fruits of many shrubs and trees, fodder crops, crop residues, crop by-products and primary products (e.g. grain).

4.1 Sources of Feed

At any given location, the ecological potential of one or more of the following sources of feed needs to be quantified by agro-ecological cells of the land resources inventory (Figure 4.1).

(i)   Grassland or pastures (permanent or long-term, or short-term grass-legume mixtures, natural or sown).

(ii)   Browse (natural woody vegetation of shrubs and trees).

(iii)   Fodder from bush and managed fallows within crop rotations (natural or sown grass-legume mixture).

(iv)   Fodder crops of fodder grasses, legumes and cereals (sown).

(v)   Fodder trees (sown).

(vi)   Fodder from fuelwood trees (sown).

(vii)   Crop residues.

(viii) Crop by-products.

(ix)   Crop primary products.

Feed supplies from each of these sources are described hereunder.

FIGURE 4.1
Sources of feed supply

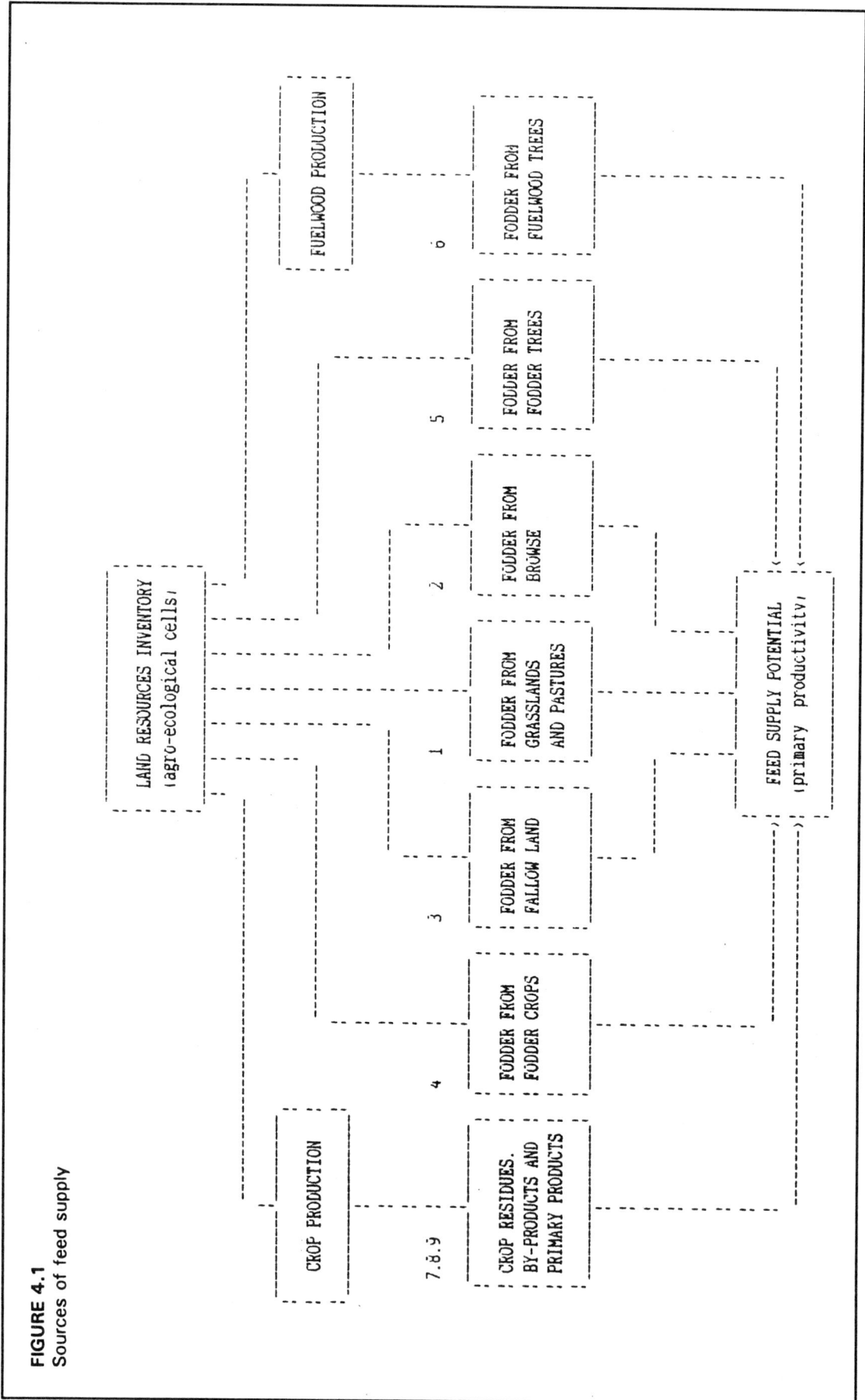

4.2 Grasslands and Pastures

Biomass production potential from grasslands or pastures in the model is estimated using the FAO-AEZ method (FAO 1978), and involves the following activities (Figure 4.2):

(i)   Selection of the species and definition of land utilization types (LUTs) (e.g. species; produce; technology and input level; labour; capital; markets).

(ii) Determination of climatic requirements of species and LUTs and matching climatic requirements with the characteristics of the inventoried climatic zones (thermal zones and growing period zones), and quantifying the climatically attainable yield potentials.

(iii) Determination of edaphic (soil) requirements of species and LUTs, and matching edaphic requirements with the characteristics of the inventoried soil units, textures, phases and stoniness to rate edaphic limitations.

(iv) Quantifying soil erosion hazards (soil loss) in each climate-soil unit (agro-ecological cell) of the land resources inventory by LUT and the associated productivity losses.

(v)   Modifying the climatic yield potentials (in ii) according to the soil limitations (in iii) and erosion hazards (in iv) to quantify yield potentials with constraints and ecological land suitabilities of each inventoried climate-soil land unit for each LUT.

Each of these activities is described in the following sections.

4.2.1 *Land utilization types*

Considerable work has been done on screening pasture (and fodder grass and legume species) to determine those best suited to particular environments in Kenya (Edwards and Bogdan 1951; Rattray 1960; Pratt and Gwynne 1977; Boonman 1979; Jaetzhold and Schmidt 1982). Table 4.1 sets out a list of some of these pasture (and fodder species) that are considered suitable in Kenya.

Pasture production is considered at three levels of inputs. The attributes of the three levels of inputs circumstances are listed in Table 4.2, and they form the basis of the definition of land utilization types considered in the model.

4.2.2 *Climatic inventory*

The climatic resources inventory of Kenya (Technical Annex 1) quantifies both heat and moisture conditions.

The quantification of heat attributes has been achieved by defining reference thermal zones representing the prevailing temperature regimes[1]. Temperature seasonality effects of latitude are minor due to the equatorial position of Kenya.

---

[1]   The following equation closely represents the relationship between average annual daily temperature in degrees Celcius (T) and altitude in metres (A): T = 30.2 - 6.496(A/1000).

FIGURE 4.2
Schematic presentation of suitability assessment for grassland/pasture

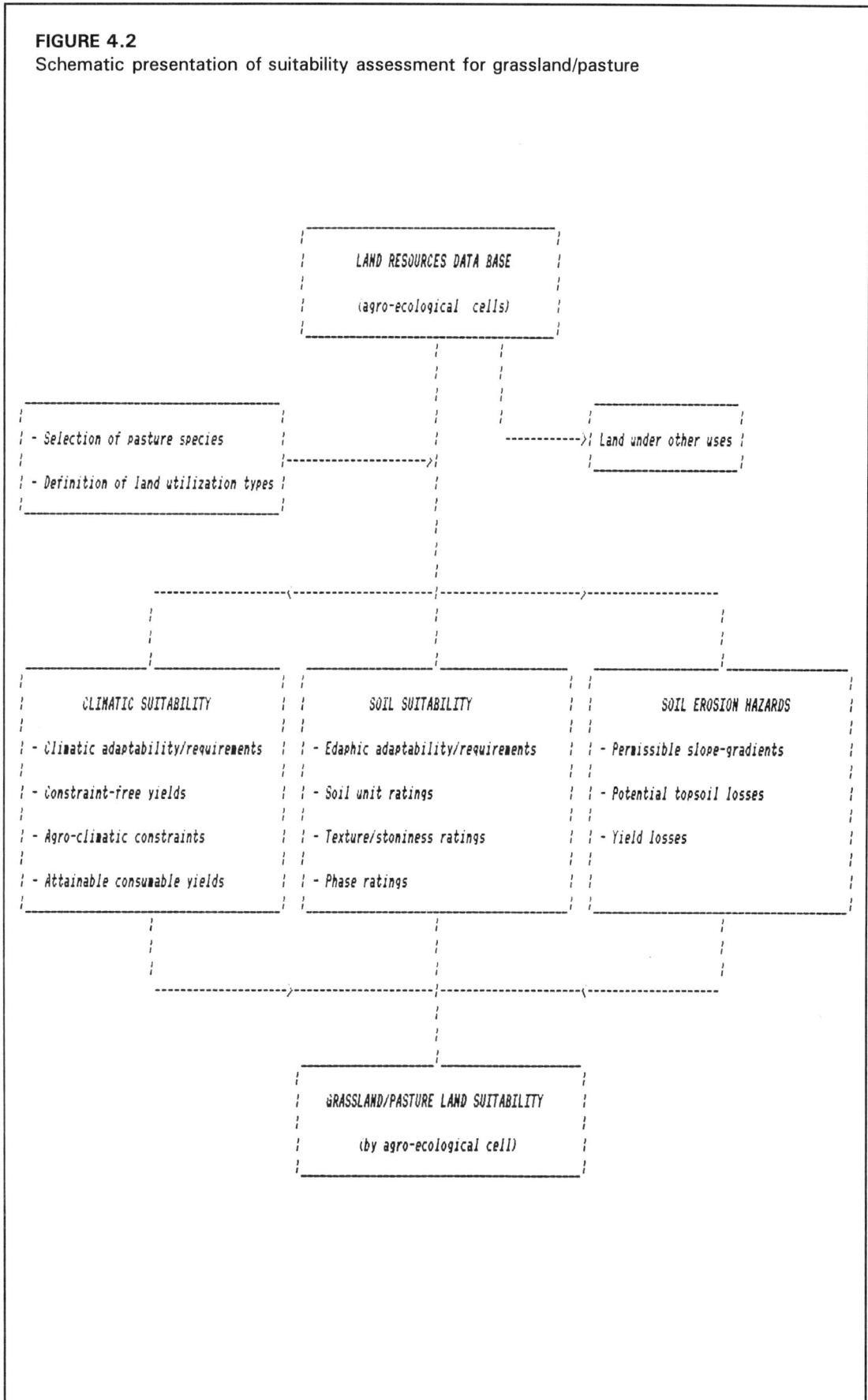

TABLE 4.1
Pasture and fodder species of grasses and legumes

Species name		Common name
Grasses:		
1	*Aristida* spp.	
2	*Cenchrus ciliaris*	Buffel grass
3	*Chloris gayana*	Rhodes grass
4	*Cynodon dactylon*	Star grass (Bermuda grass)
5	*Dactylis glomerata*	Cocksfoot (Orchard grass)
6	*Digitaria* spp.	
7	*Eragrostis superba*	Masai lovegrass
8	*Exotheca abyssinica*[1]	Exotheca
9	*Fescue* spp.	Fescue grass
10	*Hyperrhenia* spp.[1]	Zebra grass
11	*Lolium* spp.	Rye grass
12	*Melinis minutiflora*	Molasses grass
13	*Panicum coloratum*	Coloured Guinea grass
14	*Panicum maximum*	Guinea grass
15	*Pennisetum catabasis*[1]	
16	*Pennisetum clandestinum*	Kikuyu grass
17	*Pennisetum purpureum*[2]	Napier grass (Elephant grass)
18	*Pennisetum schimperi*	
19	*Setaria sphacelata*	Golden timothy
20	*Setaria splendida*[2]	Giant setaria
21	*Sorghum sudanense*[2]	Sudan grass
22	*Sporobolus helvolus*[1]	
23	*Themeda triandra*	Red oat grass
24	*Tripsacum laxacum*[2]	Guatemala grass
Legumes:		
25	*Centrosema pubescens*[2]	
26	*Desmodium* spp.[3]	Tick clover
27	*Lablab purpureus*[2]	Hyacinth bean
28	*Medicago sativa*[2]	Lucerne or alfalfa
29	*Macroptilium atropurpureum*[3]	Siratro
30	*Stylosanthes* spp.	Stylo
31	*Trifolium* spp.	Clover
32	*Vigna* spp.[2]	

[1] Common in areas of impede drainage or in seasonally waterlogged areas.
[2] Fodder species.
[3] Includes pasture and fodder types.

To cater for differences in temperature adaptability between species nine thermal zones (based on 2.5°C intervals) are distinguished in the climatic inventory of Kenya (Table 4.3). The temperature threshold values used in these definitions accord with those differentiating the four temperature adaptability groups of crop, pasture and tree species described in Technical Annexes 3, 4 and 6, and in Section 4.2.3.

Quantification of moisture conditions was achieved through the concept of reference length of growing period (LGP), being defined as the duration (in days) when moisture supply can permit crop growth. A moisture supply from rainfall of half, or more than half, potential evapotranspiration has been considered to permit crop growth. The following main concepts, definitions and methods form the basis of the quantification of moisture conditions in the climatic inventory.

TABLE 4.2
Attributes of land utilization types considered for production of pasture and fodder grasses and legumes

Attributes	Low inputs	Intermediate inputs	High inputs
Primary resource	Natural vegetation	Eradication of unpalatable species. Legumes introduced into grassland in zones with >30 days growing period together with selective clearing. Fodder crops and legume sod seeding introduced in zones with >90 days growing period.	Eradication of unpalatable species. Legumes introduced into grassland in zones with >30 days growing period together with selective clearing. Fodder cultivation and legume sod seeding in zones with >90 days growing period.
Water	Surface water, shallow well (lifted by hand)	Boreholes and deep lined wells (windmill/engine driven pumps).	Adequate water reticulation (windmill/engine: gravity distribution).
Land use and feeding system	Traditional (extensive): permanent grazing; no fire control	Controlled (semi-intensive): group ranching; rotational grazing + stall feeding; fire partially controlled; fodder conservation for dry season.	Controlled (intensive): control of numbers and movement; rotational semi-zero and zero grazing; fire controlled; fodder conservation for dry season.
Fertilization	None	In conjunction with legume introduction in region with >90 days growing period application of ground rock phosphate and thiobacillus or superphosphate. With fodder crops, intermediate levels of plant nutrients from fertilizer and manure.	Optimum amount plant nutrients.
Herding	Traditional	Organized	Use of hedges and fences.

Table 4.3
Thermal zones

Thermal zone code	Temperature class (°C)	Altitude (m)
1	> 25.0	< 800
2	22.5 - 25.0	800 - 1200
3	20.0 - 22.5	1200 - 1550
4	17.5 - 20.0	1550 - 1950
5	15.0 - 17.5	1950 - 2350
6	12.5 - 15.0	2350 - 2700
7	10.0 - 12.5	2700 - 3100
8	5.0 - 10.0	3100 - 3900
9	< 5.0	> 3900

The growing period is the time when moisture supply from rainfall exceeds half potential evapotranspiration. It includes the time required to evapotranspire up to 100 mm of stored moisture from the soil profile. A 'normal' growing period has a humid phase, i.e. a period when moisture supply is greater than full potential evapotranspiration. When there is no humid period, the growing period is defined as 'intermediate'.

The quantification of moisture regime is based on the analysis of the length of growing period for each year seperately and the computation of:

(a)   number of seperate lengths of growing periods per year, summerized as a historical profile of **pattern of number of length of growing periods per year (LGP-Pattern)**;

(b)   length of each growing period and its various moisture periods, summarized as mean total dominant length, first associated length and second associated length, and the mean individual dominant and associated lengths making up the total lengths;

(c)   the quality of moisture conditions during the growing period and its various moisture periods;

(d)   year-to-year variability (frequency distribution) of each length of growing period and the associated moisture condition.

Twenty two LGP-Patterns are recognized, and these with their composition are presented in Table 4.4. The LGP-Pattern code represents the number of growing periods per year in order of frequency of occurrence, e.g. in the pattern coded 2-1-3, the numeral 2 represents the number of lengths of growing periods per year (i.e. two) that occur in the majority of the years (i.e. 55 percent) - the dominant length number; the numeral 1 represents number of lengths of growing periods per year (i.e. one) that has the next most commonly occurring frequency (i.e. 25 percent) - the first associated length number; and the numeral 3 represents number of lengths of growing periods per year (i.e. three) that has the smallest occurrence (i.e. 20 percent) - the second associated length number.

For each LGP-Pattern type, the mean total length of the dominant number is correlated with the mean total length of the associated numbers. Also, when the mean total length is a summation of more than one mean length, the latter lengths are again correlated with the former total length. These relationships are presented in Tables 4.5 and 4.6.

In the climatic inventory of Kenya, only the mean total dominant length has been inventoried on the map as 15 LGP zones. The boundary or isoline values used are 0, 30, 60, 90, 120, 150, 180, 210, 240, 270, 300, 330, 365$^-$ and 365$^+$ days respectively delineating the mean total dominant length of growing period zones of 0, 1-29, 30-59, 60-89, 90-119, 120-149, 150-179, 180-209, 210-239, 240-269, 270-299, 300-329, 330-364, 365^{-1} and 365^{+2} days.

---

1   365$^-$ - year round growing priod but not humid year-round.

2   365$^+$ - year-round humid growing period.

TABLE 4.4
Patterns of growing periods (LGP-patterns) - Historical profiles of occurrence of number of length of growing periods per year

Code	LGP-pattern	Proportion (%)
1	1	100
2	H - 1	60 : 40
3	1 - H	70 : 30
4	1 - H - 2	65 : 20 : 15
5	1 - 2 - H	65 : 20 : 15
6	1 - 2	65 : 35
7	1 - 2 - 3	50 : 35 : 15
8	1 - 3 - 2	40 : 35 : 20
9	1 - 2 - D	40 : 35 : 25
10	1 - D - 2	40 : 35 : 25
11	1 - D	60 : 40
12	2	100
13	2 - 1	70 : 30
14	2 - 1 - H	55 : 30 : 15
15	2 - 1 - 3	55 : 25 : 20
16	2 - 3	75 : 25
17	2 - 3 - 1	60 : 25 : 15
18	2 - 3 - 4	50 : 30 : 10
19	2 - 1 - D	70 : 15 : 15
20	3 - 2	60 : 40
21	3 - 2 - 1	50 : 35 : 15
22	D	100

H = 365$^+$ days (i.e. year-round humid)
D = zero days (i.e. year-round dry)

TABLE 4.5
Relationships between mean total dominant and mean total associated lengths of growing period

LGP-Pattern	Relationship
1 - 2 1 - 2 - H 1 - H - 2	L2 = 80.40 + 0.75 L1
1 - 2 - 3 1 - 3 - 2 1 - 2 - D 1 - 2 - D	L2 = 71.56 + 0.66 L1 L3 = 77.14 + 0.66 L1
2 - 1 2 - 1 - H 2 - 1 - 3 2 - 1 - D	L1 = -86.09 + 1.28 L2 L3 = 25.29 + 0.82 L2
2 - 3 2 - 3 - 1 2 - 3 - 4	L3 = 30.11 + 0.83 L2 L1 = -98.72 + 1.35 L2 L4 = 114.54 + 0.58 L2
3 - 2 3 - 2 - 1	L2 = 45.05 + 0.80 L3 L1 = -9.86 + 0.88 L3

L1 = Total length of one growing period per year
L2 = Total length of two growing periods per year
L3 = Total length of three growing periods per year
L4 = Total length of four growing periods per year

Additionally, the LGP-Pattern zones have been inventoried. Consequently, the relationships in Tables 4.5 and 4.6 together with the map of dominant LGP zones and the LGP-Pattern zones provide the historical profile of any mean total dominant length of growing period in any of the 22 LGP-Pattern zones.

Reference tables relating the mean total dominant LGPs (mapped) and the corresponding mean total associated LGPs (unmapped) are presented in Technical Annex 1, together with generalized coefficients of variation of mean LGPs, and frequency of occurrence of intermediate LGPs.

4.2.3 *Climatic suitability*

Climatic suitability assessment of grass and legume pasture species is based on the climatic adaptability principles described in FAO (1978), and includes:

(a) An understanding of the climatic adaptability of pasture species in terms of their ecophysiological characteristics.

(b) Matching the climatic requirements to thermal and moisture regimes, including the estimation of constraint-free biomass potentials.

(c) Rating of agro-climatic constraints of water stress/excess; pests, diseases and weeds; and workability.

(d) Estimating attainable biomass production potentials with constraints, and the consumable biomass fractions.

The list of grass and legume species given in Table 4.1 includes both C^4 species (grasses) and C^3 species (legumes). Both groups of species include ecotypes that are adapted to operate under warmer (mean daily temperature $> 20°C$) as well as cooler (mean daily temperature $<20°C$) conditions. Table 4.7 presents the thermal zone screen for pasture and fodder species showing which species can be considered in which thermal zones.

Legume species adapted to operate under cool temperatures ($<20°C$ mean daily temperature) belong to adaptability group I, and those adapted to operate under warm temperatures ($>20°C$) belong to adaptability group II. Grass species adapted to operate under warm temperatures ($>20°C$) belong to adaptability group III, and those adapted to operate under cool temperatures ($<20°C$) belong to adaptability group IV. The relationships between photosynthesis and temperature for the four adaptability groups are presented in Table 4.8.

TABLE 4.6

Relationship between individual component mean length and mean total length of growing period

LGP-Pattern	Relationship
2 1 - 2 1 - 2 - H 1 - H - 2	$L2_1 = -1.11 + 0.55 \, L2$ $L2_1 = 4.94 + 0.62 \, L2$
1 - 2 - 3 1 - 3 - 2 1 - 2 - D 1 - D - 2	$L2_1 = 5.87 + 0.64 \, L2$ $L3_1 = 22.12 + 0.39 \, L3$ $L3_2 = 1.58 + 0.32 \, L3$
2 - 1 2 - 1 - H 2 - 1 - 3 2 - 1 - D	$L2_1 = -5.48 + 0.64 \, L2$ $L3_1 = 0.14 + 0.46 \, L3$ $L3_2 = -0.98 + 0.33 \, L3$
2 - 3 2 - 3 - 1 2 - 3 - 4	$L2_1 = -3.05 + 0.61 \, L2$ $L3_1 = 1.68 + 0.43 \, L3$ $L3_2 = -3.00 + 0.34 \, L3$ $L4_1 = 26.35 + 0.34 \, L4$ $L4_2 = -20.88 + 0.38 \, L4$ $L4_3 = -17.66 + 0.27 \, L4$
3 - 2 3 - 2 - 1	$L2_1 = -2.33 + 0.63 \, L2$ $L3_1 = 5.62 + 0.45 \, L3$ $L3_2 = 1.25 + 0.31 \, L3$

$L2_1$ = First length of two growing periods per year
$L3_1$ = First length of three growing periods per year
$L3_2$ = Second length of three growing periods per year
$L4_1$ = First length of four growing periods per year
$L4_2$ = Second length of four growing periods per year
$L4_3$ = Third length of four growing periods per year

Consequently, the suggested thermal zone combination ratings for the grasses and legumes at this stage of the model development are: S1 (very suitable) for the thermal zones T1, T2, T3, T4 and T5, S2 (suitable) for T6, S3 (moderately suitable) for T7, S4 (marginally suitable) for T8 and N (not suitable) for T9. A rating of S1 indicates that there are no thermal constraints during the growing period and the requirements are fully met. A rating of S2 indicates slight to moderate thermal constraints leading to yield supressions of some 25 %. A rating of S3 indicates that there are moderate to severe thermal constraints leading to yield suppressions of some 50%. A rating of S4 indicates severe thermal constraints leading to yield suppressions of some 75%. A rating of N indicates that the thermal requirements are not met and the zone is not suitable for further consideration. These ratings correspond closely with the correlation between pasture dry matter production and temperature in Kenya (Booneman 1979).

TABLE 4.7
Thermal zone screen for pasture and fodder species

Species name	Adaptability group	Thermal zone							
		T1	T2	T3	T4	T5	T6	T7	T8
Grasses:									
1 *Aristida* spp.	III	•	•	•					
2 *Cenchrus ciliaris*	III	•	•	•	•				
3 *Chloris gayana*	III, IV	•	•	•	•	•			
4 *Cynodon dactylon*	III, IV	•	•	•	•	•	•		
5 *Dactylis glomerata*	IV					•	•	•	•
6 *Digitaria* spp.	III	•	•	•	•				
7 *Eragrostis superba*	III	•	•	•	•				
8 *Exotheca abyssinica*	IV			•	•	•	•		
9 *Festuca* spp.	IV					•	•	•	•
10 *Hyperrhenia* spp.	III, IV	•	•	•	•	•	•		
11 *Lolium* spp.	IV					•	•	•	•
12 *Melinis minutiflora*	III, IV			•	•	•	•		
13 *Panicum coloratum*	III, IV	•	•	•	•	•			
14 *Panicum maximum*	III, IV	•	•	•	•	•			
15 *Pennisetum catabasis*	IV			•	•	•	•		
16 *Pennisetum clandestinum*	IV			•	•	•	•		
17 *Pennisetum purpureum*	III, IV		•	•	•	•			
18 *Pennisetum schimperi*	IV			•	•	•	•	•	•
19 *Setaria sphacelata*	III, IV			•	•	•	•		
20 *Setaria splendida*	III, IV	•	•	•	•	•			
21 *Sorghum sudanense*	III, IV	•	•	•	•	•			
22 *Sporobolus helvolus*	III	•	•	•					
23 *Themeda triandra*	IV			•	•	•	•	•	•
24 *Tripsacum laxacum*	III, IV	•	•	•	•	•			
Legumes:									
25 *Centrosema pubescens*	II	•	•	•					
26 *Desmodium* spp.	II	•	•	•					
27 *Lablab purpureus*	II	•	•	•					
28 *Medicago sativa*	I				•	•	•	•	•
29 *Macroptilium atropurpureum*	II	•	•	•					
30 *Stylosanthes* spp.	II	•	•	•	•		•	•	•
31 *Trifolium* spp.	I				•	•			
32 *Vigna* spp.	II	•	•	•					

TABLE 4.8
Relationships between temperature and rate of leaf photosynthesis (kg CH$_2$O/ha/hr) for legume species in adaptability groups I and II, and grass species in adaptability groups III and IV

Adaptability group	Temperature (°C)							
	5	10	15	20	25	30	35	40
Legume I	2.5	10.0	20.0	25.0	25.0	20.0	10.0	5.0
Legume II	-	2.5	15.0	35.0	37.5	37.5	30.0	20.0
Grass III	-	2.5	30.0	40.0	50.0	50.0	47.5	40.0
Grass IV	2.5	15.0	37.5	50.0	50.0	37.5	25.0	10.0

Potential biomass estimates were derived according to the method developed by the FAO-AEZ project (Kassam 1977; FAO 1978-81). For the purpose of computing ' constraint-free' biomass potential, it is assumed that both C_3 and C_4 pasture and fodder species of grasses and legumes will be represented, so that maximum photosynthesis rate (Pm) of 37.5 CH_2O ha^{-1} hr^{-1} has been applied.

Estimates of constraint-free total biomass (Bn) at high level of inputs are presented in Table 4.9 together with maximum leaf area index (LAI) values used, the agro-climatic constraint ratings, total biomass with constraints (Bnc), consumable coefficients (Cc) and consumable biomass with constraints (Bcc).

For a variety of reasons only a portion of the plant biomass is eaten by animals. About 20% of the total net biomass (Bn) is in roots, a portion of the biomass is not eaten (particularly under low inputs) due to low palatability; some biomass is lost due to trampling, fire and wind, and part is consumed by invertebrate animals. It is generally assumed that between a third and two-thirds of the total biomass yield of an area will be utilized or consumed by stock, depending on the environment.

Agro-climatic constraints applied to the constraint-free yield relate to water stress in LGP < 210 days and workability in LGP zone 365^+ days. Total biomass yield with constraint at high inputs range from 0.5 t/ha in LGP zone 1-29 days to 30.6 t/ha in LGP zone 330-364 days.

Consumable coefficients (Cc) range from 0.35 at low inputs in LGP zones with < 120 days to 0.6 at high inputs in LGP zones with > 180 days. Consequently, consumable biomass with constraints (Bcc) range from 0.23 t/ha to 18.9 t/ha for high inputs, from 0.16 to 10.83 t/ha for intermediate inputs, and from 0.09 t/ha to 3.94 t/ha for low inputs.

Constraint-free net biomass (Bn) at low inputs is assumed to be 25% and 50% of those at high input level in the LGP zones > 90 days and < 90 days respectively. Constraint-free total biomass at intermediate level is assumed to be between the high and the low input levels. For areas with no growing period Bc is estimated at 70 kg/ha at the high inputs level and 35 kg/ha at the low and 52.5 kg/ha at the intermediate inputs level.

Pasture species and biomass potentials are matched to individual component length of growing periods, i.e. L1, $L2_1$, $L2_2$, $L3_1$, $L3_2$, $L3_3$, $L4_1$, $L4_2$, $L4_3$, $L4_4$. The LGP-Pattern evaluation for pasture is achieved by taking into account all the constituent component lengths in each LGP-Pattern, thus taking into account the year-to-year variability in the number of LGPs per year.

Yields in Table 4.9 apply to normal lengths of growing periods. For intermediate growing periods, yield reductions are of the order of 50% on all soils except Fluvisols and Gleysols. The percentage of occurrence of intermediate lengths of growing periods in all LGP-Pattern zones combined is 100% in LGP zone 1-29 days; 65% in zone 30-59 days; 25% in zone 60-89 days; 10% in zone 90-119 days and 5% in zone 120-149 days.

An exception to the general methodology for climatic suitability assessment applies to areas occupied by Fluvisols because the inventoried length of growing period does not fully reflect their particular circumstances with regards to moisture regime.

TABLE 4.9

Potential biomass from pasture and fodder grasses and legumes (t/ha dry weight) at three input levels[1]

	1-29	30-59	60-89	90-119	120-149	150-179	180-209	210-239	240-269	270-299	300-329	330-364	365	365+
LAI	1-2	2-3	3-4	4	4	4	4	4	4	4	4	4	4	4
Bn	0.0-1.8	1.8-5.3	5.3-10.0	10.0-14.3	14.3-17.2	17.2-19.7	19.7-22.1	22.1-24.3	24.3-26.3	26.3-28.2	28.2-29.7	29.7-31.5	31.5	31.5
a[1]	2	2	2	1	1	1	1	0	0	0	0	0	0	0
b	0	0	0	0	0	0	0	0	0	0	0	0	0	0
c	0	0	0	0	0	0	0	0	0	0	0	0	0	0
d	0	0	0	0	0	0	0	0	0	0	0	0	0	1
Bnc	0.5	1.8	3.8	9.1	11.8	13.8	15.7	23.2	25.3	27.3	29.0	30.6	31.5	23.6
Cc — H[2]	0.45	0.45	0.45	0.45	0.50	0.50	0.60	0.60	0.60	0.60	0.60	0.60	0.60	0.60
— I	0.40	0.40	0.40	0.40	0.45	0.55	0.55	0.55	0.55	0.55	0.55	0.55	0.55	0.55
— L	0.35	0.35	0.35	0.35	0.40	0.50	0.50	0.50	0.50	0.50	0.50	0.50	0.50	0.50
Bcc — H	0.23	0.81	1.71	4.10	5.90	6.80	9.42	13.92	15.18	16.38	17.40	18.36	18.90	14.16
— I	0.16	0.54	1.14	2.28	3.32	3.88	5.40	7.98	8.70	9.38	9.97	10.52	10.83	8.07
— L	0.09	0.32	0.67	0.80	1.18	1.38	1.96	2.90	3.16	3.41	3.63	3.82	3.94	2.96

1   Agroclimatic constraints: a = water stress or excess; b = pests, diseases or weeds affecting reproductive growth; c = pests, diseases or weeds affecting vegetative growth; d = workability limitations.

2   H = high inputs; I = intermediate inputs; L = low inputs.

TABLE 4.10
Fluvisols ratings by length of growing period (days) at high, intermediate and low levels of inputs

Inputs level	Growth period (days)	Maxi-mum yield (t/ha)	Length of growing period							
			0	1-29	30-59	60-89	90-119	120-149	150-179	180-209
High	30-365	18.90	S6	S5	S4	S4	S3	S3	S2	S2
Intermediate	30-365	10.83	S6	S5	S4	S4	S3	S3	S2	S2
Low	30-365	3.94	S6	S5	S4	S4	S3	S3	S2	S2

Inputs level	Growth period (days)	Maxi-mum yield (t/ha)	Length of growing period						
			210-239	240-269	270-299	300-329	330-364	365⁻	365⁺
High	30-365	18.90	S2	S3	S4	S4	S4	S4	S5
Intermediate	30-365	10.83	S2	S3	S4	S4	S4	S4	S5
Low	30-365	3.94	S2	S3	S4	S4	S4	S4	S5

Land use on Fluvisols is generally governed by the depth, intensity and duration of flooding which occurs in the low lying areas of these soils. These flooding attributes are generally controlled not by the amount of 'on site' rainfall but by external factors of catchment area and catchment-site relationships.

Fluvisols ratings are presented in Table 4.10 for the three levels of inputs circumstances. Suitability ratings S1, S2, S3, S4, S5, S6 and N, correspond to potential biomass yield supressions of zero, 25%, 50%, 75%, 90%, 95% and 100% respectively.

4.2.4 *An example of biomass calculation*

An example of the calculation of constraint-free total net biomass and constraint-free consumable biomass for Lamu (with thermal suitability S1) is presented below.

Net biomass (Bn) is calculated from the equation:

$$Bn = (0.36 \; bgm \times L) \, / \, (1/N + 0.25 \; Ct) \qquad (4.1)$$

where:

bgm = maximum rate of gross biomass production at leaf area index (LAI) of 5 (kg CH_2O ha^{-1} day^{-1})

L = maximum growth ratio, equal to the ratio of bgm at actual LAI to bgm at LAI of 5. (L at LAI 1, 2, 3, 4 and 5 is 0.4, 0.6, 0.8, 0.9 and 1.0 respectively)

N = length of crop growth cycle (days)

Ct = maintenance respiration coefficient, dependent on both crop and temperature; given by the relation:

$$Ct = C30 \; (0.0044 + 0.0019 \; T + 0.0010 \; T^2)$$

At 30 °C, C = 0.0283 for a legume species and 0.0108 for a non-legume species.

Table 4.11

Photosynthetically active radiation on very clear days (ac) in cal cm^{-2} day^{-1} and the daily gross photosynthesis rate of standard crop canopies on very clear (bc) and overcast (bo) days in kg CH$_2$O ha^{-1} day^{-1} for Pm = 20 kg CH$_2$O ha^{-1} hr^{-1} (from De Wit 1965)

Lat. North		Jan	Feb	Mar	Apr	May	Jun	Jul	Aug	Sep	Oct	Nov	Dec
Lat. South		Jul	Aug	Sep	Oct	Nov	Dec	Jan	Feb	Mar	Apr	May	Jun
0°	Ac	343	360	369	364	349	337	342	357	368	365	349	337
	bc	413	424	429	426	417	410	413	422	429	427	418	410
	bo	219	226	230	228	221	216	218	225	230	228	222	216
10°	Ac	299	332	359	375	377	374	375	377	369	345	311	291
	bc	376	401	422	437	440	440	440	439	431	411	385	370
	bo	197	212	225	234	236	235	236	235	230	218	203	193

Constraint-free consumable biomass (Bc) is calculated from constraint-free total net biomass (Bn) from the equation:

$$Bc = Cc \times Bn \qquad (4.2)$$

where: Cc = Consumable coefficient, i.e. consumable portion of the total net biomass Bn (equivalent to harvest index in field crops).

The maximum rate of gross biomass production (bgm) is dependent on the maximum photosynthesis (Pm) which is dependent on temperature and photosynthesis pathway of the crop. Maximum rates of photosynthesis (Pm) for pasture species of grasses and legumes is taken as 37.5 kg CH$_2$O ha^{-1} hr^{-1} (Table 4.8).

For Pm = 20 kg CH$_2$O ha^{-1} hr^{-1} and LAI of 5, bgm is calculated from the equation:

$$bgm = F \times bo + (1-F) bc \qquad (4.3)$$

where:

F = fraction of the daytime the sky is clouded:

F = (Ac - 0.5 Rg)/(0.8 Ac) where Ac is the maximum active incoming shortwave radiation on clear days in cal cm^{-2} day^{-1} (Table 4.11) and Rg is the incoming shortwave radiation in cal cm^{-2} day^{-1}

bo = gross dry matter production rate of a standard crop for a given location on a completely overcast day, kg CH$_2$O ha^{-1} day^{-1} (Table 4.11)

bc = gross dry matter production rate of standard crop for a given location on a clear (cloudless) day, kg CH$_2$O ha^{-1} day^{-1} (Table 4.11).

When Pm is greater than 20 kg CH$_2$O ha^{-1} hr^{-1}, bgm is given by the equation:

$$bgm = F(0.8 + 0.01 Pm)bo + (1 - F)(0.5 + 0.025Pm)bc. \qquad (4.4)$$

When Pm is less than 20 kg CH$_2$O ha^{-1} hr^{-1}, bgm is given by the equation:

$$bgm = F(0.5 + 0.025Pm)bo + (1 - F)(0.05Pm)bc. \qquad (4.5)$$

Climate:

Station: Lamu
Location: 2° 16' S and 40° 54' E
Altitude: 30 m
Growing period: 140 days
Start growing period: 5 April
End growing period: 25 August
Average radiation (Rg): 471 cal cm^{-2} day
Average day-time temperature: 26.5 °C
Average 24hr mean temperature: 25.3 °C

Species adaptability:

Pasture species (grasses and legumes)
Growth cycle: 140 days (equal to growing period)
Leaf area index at maximum growth rate: 4
Consumable coefficient: 0.50
Species adaptability: Photosynthesis pathway C_3/C_4, groups II and III

Calculation of rate of gross biomass production (bgm)

Photosynthesis rate Pm at 26.5 °C: 37.5 kg CH_2O ha^{-1} hr^{-1}.

Difference in Pm relative to Pm = 20 kg CH_2O ha^{-1} hr^{-1}: 87.5%.

Average photosynthetically active radiation on clear days (Ac) : 351 cal cm^{-2} day^{-1} (Table 4.11).

Fraction of the day-time when the sky is overcast (F): 0.41 (from equation F = (Ac - 0.5Rg)/0.8Ac).

Average rate of gross biomass production for perfectly clear days at Pm = 20 kg CH_2O ha^{-1} hr^{-1} (bc): 418 kg CH_2O ha^{-1} hr^{-1} (Table 4.11).

Average rate of gross biomass production for totally overcast days at Pm = 20 kg CH_2O ha^{-1} hr^{-1} (bo): 222 kg CH_2O ha^{-1} hr^{-1} (Table 4.11).

Rate of gross biomass production at Pm = 20 kg CH_2O ha^{-1} hr^{-1} at LAI of 5 : 324 kg CH_2O ha^{-1} day^{-1} (from equation 4.3).

Rate of gross biomass production at Pm = 35 kg CH_2O ha^{-1} hr^{-1} at LAI of 5 (bgm): 426 kg CH_2O ha^{-1} day^{-1} (from equations 4.3 and 4.4), and 383 kg CH_2O ha^{-1} day^{-1} at LAI of 4.

Calculation of total constraint-free net biomass production (Bn) and constraint-free consumable biomass (Bc)

Maintenance respiration coefficient at 30 °C: 0.0196 (for mixture of legumes and non-legumes).

TABLE 4.12
Soil units

Symbol	Name	Symbol	Name	Symbol	Name
A	Acrisols	Gm	Mollic Gleysols	Od	Dystric Histosols
Ac	Chromic Acrisols	Gv	Vertic Gleysols	Q	Arenosols
Ag	Gleyic Acrisols	Hg	Gleyic Phaeozems	Qa	Albic Arenosols
Ah	Humic Acrisols	Hh	Haplic Phaeozems	Qc	Cambic Arenosols
Aic	Ferralo-chromic Acrisols	Hnl	Nito-luvic Phaeozems	Qf	Ferralic Arenosols
Aif	Ferralo-ferric Acrisols	Hol	Orthic-luvic Phaeozems	Qkc	Calcaro-cambic
Aio	Ferralo-orthic Acrisols	Hrl	Chromic-luvic Phaeozems		Arenosols
Ao	Orthic Acrisols	Hth	Ando-haplic Phaeozems	Ql	Luvic Arenosols
Ap	Plinthic Acrisols	Htl	Ando-luvic Phaeozems	R	Regosols
Ath	Ando-humic Acrisols	Hvl	Verto-luvic Phaeozems	Rc	Calcaric Regosols
B	Cambisols	I	Lithosols	Rd	Dystric Regosols
Bc	Chromic Cambisols	Ir	Ironstone soils	Re	Eutric Regosols
Bd	Dystric Cambisols	J	Fluvisols	Rtc	Ando-calcaric Regosols
Be	Eutric Cambisols	Jc	Calcaric Fluvisols	S	Solonetz
Bf	Ferralic Cambisols	Je	Eutric Fluvisols	Sg	Gleyic Solonetz
Bg	Gleyic Cambisols	Jt	Thionic Fluvisols	Slo	Luvo-orthic Solonetz
Bh	Humic Cambisols	Kh	Haplic Kastanozems	Sm	Mollic Solonetz
Bk	Calcic Cambisols	L	Luvisols	So	Orthic Solonetz
Bnc	Nito-chromic Cambisols	La	Albic Luvisols	Th	Humic Andosols
Btc	Ando-chromic Cambisols	Lc	Chromic Luvisols	Tm	Mollic Andosols
Bte	Ando-eutric Cambisols	Lf	Ferric Luvisols	Tv	Vitric Andosols
Bv	Vertic Cambisols	Lg	Gleyic Luvisols	U	Rankers
Ch	Haplic Chernozems	Lic	Ferralo-chromic Luvisols	V	Vertisols
Ck	Calcic Chernozems	Lif	Ferralo-ferric Luvisols	Vc	Chromic Vertisols
Ec	Cambic Renzinas	Lio	Ferralo-orthic Luvisols	Vp	Pellic Vertisols
Eo	Orthic Renzinas	Lk	Calcic Luvisols	W	Planosols
F	Ferralsols	Lnc	Nito-chromic Luvisols	Wd	Dystric Planosols
Fa	Acric Ferralsols	Lnf	Nito-ferric Luvisols	We	Eutric Planosols
Fh	Humic Ferralsols	Lo	Orthic Luvisols	Wh	Humic Planosols
Fnh	Nito-humic Ferralsols	Lv	Vertic Luvisols	Ws	Solodic Planosols
Fnr	Nito-rodic Ferralsols	Mo	Orthic Greyzems	Wve	Verto-eutric Planosols
Fo	Orthic Ferralsols	Mvo	Verto-orthic Greyzems	X	Xerosols/Yermosols
Fr	Rodic Ferralsols	Nd	Dystric Nitosols	Xh	Haplic Xero/Yermosols
Fx	Xanthic Ferralsols	Ne	Eutric Nitosols	Xk	Calcic Xero/Yermosols
G	Eutric Gleysols	Nh	Humic Nitosols	Xy	Gypsic Xero/Yermosols
Gc	Clacaric Gleysols	Nm	Mollic Nitosols	Z	Solonchaks
Gd	Dystric Gleysols	Nth	Ando-humic Nitosols	Zg	Gleyic Solonchaks
Ge	Eutric Gleysols	Nve	Verto-eutric Nitosols	Zo	Orthic Solonchaks
Gh	Humic Gleysols	Nvm	Verto-mollic Nitosols	Zt	Takyric Solonchaks

Maintenance respiration coefficient at 25.3 (Ct) °C: 0.014 (from equation $C_t = C_{30}$ (0.0044 + 0.0019 T + 0.0010 T^2)

Net total biomass (Bn): 15.5 t/ha (equation 4.1).

Consumable biomass (Bc)[1]: 7.7 t/ha (equation 4.2).

4.2.5 *Soil inventory*

The soil resources of Kenya (Technical Annex 1) have been inventoried in terms of associations of soil units, and the corresponding characterization of soil textures, stoniness, phases, and slopes.

---

[1] Without agro-climatic constraints (with constraints 5.8 t/ha).

Soil units have been defined in terms of measurable and observable properties of the soil itself, and specific clusters of such properties are combined into 'diagnostic horizons' and 'diagnostic properties', which are used in the definition of the soil units. The soil units inventoried in the Kenya soil resources inventory (Exploratory Soil Map of Kenya) are listed in Table 4.12 and the diagnostic horizons and properties of these soil units are presented in the Technical Annex 1.

Soil texture may vary within the range of textures defined for a particular soil unit. In the legend of the Exploratory Soil Map, textural classes for the individual soil units by soil mapping unit are presented. The three major textural divisions (coarse, medium and fine) are subdivided into 17 classes (Table 4.13).

Soil phases indicate land characteristics which are not considered in the definition of the soil units but are significant to the use and management of land. Soil phases recognized on the Exploratory Soil Map of Kenya can be grouped into phases indicating a mechanical hindrance or limitation (rocky, bouldery, boulder-mantle, stony, stone-mantle, gravel-mantle), phases indicating an effective soil depth limitation (lithic, paralithic, petro-calcic, piso-calcic, petro-ferric, piso-ferric), and phases indicating a physico-chemical limitation (saline, sodic and saline-sodic). Soil phases occur either individually or in combinations of upto three. They are described in Technical Annex 2, and are listed in Table 4.14.

TABLE 4.13
Texture classes

Texture symbol	Texture class
Coarse:	
S	Sand
LCS	Loamy coarse sand
FS	Fine sand
LFS	Loamy fine sand
LS	Loamy sand
Medium	
FSL	Fine sandy loam
SL	Sandy loam
L	Loam
SCL	Sandy clay loam
SL	Silty loam
CL	Clay loam
SIL	Silty clay loam
SI	Silt
Fine:	
SC	Sandy clay
SIC	Silty clay
PC	Peaty clay
C	Clay

The presence of coarse material (stoniness) in the soil profile has been inventoried seperately from soil textures. Six types of coarse material or stoniness have been inventoried: Gravelly (G), Very Gravelly (VG), Stony (S), Bouldery (B), Stony/Bouldery (SB) and Bouldery/Stony (BS).

Six basic slope classes, in 12 combinations, have been employed in the Exploratory Soil Map of Kenya. The six basic slope classes are: A: 0-2%; B: 2-5%; C: 5-8%; D: 8-16%; E: 16-30% and F: > 30%. The 12 combination slope classes are: A: 0-2%; AB: 0-5%; B: 2-5%; BC: 2-8%; C: 5-8%; BCD: 2-16%; CD: 5-16%; D: 8-16%; DE: 8-30%; E: 16-30%; EF: 16->30%; F: >30%.

To each of these 12 slope classes, associated slope classes have been assigned. These associated slope classes, covering upto 10% of the land area of the 12 slope classes, are used for evaluation purposes only. They are not included explicitly in the soil resources inventory. The 12 inventoried combination slope classes and the associated slope classes are presented in Table 4.15 For the same purposes of evaluation, assumed mean slopes have been assigned to each of the quartiles of the land area of each of the 12 slope classes (Table 4.16).

TABLE 4.14
Soil phases

Symbol	Name	Symbol	Name	Symbol	Name
Single:		Combination of two:		Combination of three:	
R	Rocky	R/B	Rocky and bouldery	R/B/AO	Rocky and bouldery and saline-sodic
B	Bouldery	R/S	Rocky and stony	R/P/S	Rocky and lithic and stony
BM	Boulder-mantle	B/S	Bouldery and stony	B/S/A	Bouldery and stony and saline
S	Stony	BM/AO	Boulder-mantle and saline-sodic	BM/S/AO	Bouldery and stony and saline-sodic
SM	Stone-mantle	S/R	Stony and rocky	P/R/B	Lithic and rocky and bouldery
G	Gravelly	S/B	Stony and bouldery	P/B/S	Lithic and rocky and stony
GM	Gravel-mantle	S/K	Stony and petrocalcic	P/B/A	Lithic and bouldery and saline
P	Lithic	S/AO	Stony and saline-sodic	P/BM/AO	Lithic and bouldery-mantle and saline sodic
PP	Paralithic	SM/O	Stone-mantle and sodic	P/S/R	Lithic and stony and rocky
K	Petrocalcic	SM/AO	Stone-mantle and saline-sodic	P/S/A	Lithic and stony and saline
KK	Petrocalcic	P/R	Lithic and rocky	P/S/AO	Lithic and stony and saline-sodic
C	Pisocalcic	P/B	Lithic and bouldery	P/SM/AO	Lithic and stone-mantle and saline-sodic
CC	Pisocalcic	P/BM	Lithic and boulder-mantle	P/GM/S	Lithic and gravel-mantle and saline
M	Petroferric	P/S	Lithic and stony		
MM	Pisoferric	P/O	Lithic and sodic		
A	Saline	P/AO	Lithic and saline-sodic		
O	Sodic	PP/R	Paralithic and rocky		
AO	Saline-sodic	PP/S	Paralithic and stony		
F	Fragipan	K/S	Petrocalcic and stony		
		K/A	Petrocalcic and saline-sodic		
		KK/A	Petrocalcic and saline		
		KK/O	Petrocalcic and sodic		
		N/R	Pisoferric and rocky		
		N/M	Pisoferric and pisoferric		
		A/F	Pisoferric and fragipan		
		O/F	Sodic and fragipan		

TABLE 4.15
Associated slope classes

Slope class		Associated slope classes		
Symbol	%			
A	0 - 2	100% A		
AB	0 - 5	100% AB		
B	2 - 5	100% B		
BC	2 - 8	90% BC	5% A	
C	5 - 8	90% C	5% AB	5% D
BCD	2 - 16	90% BCD	5% A	5% D
CD	5 - 16	90% CD	5% AB	5% E
D	8 - 16	90% D	5% BC	5% E
DE	8 - 30	90% DE	5% BC	5% E
E	16 - 30	90% E	5% BCD	5% F
EF	16 - 56	95% EF	5% BCD	5% F
F	30 - 56	95% F	5% DE	

4.2.6 *Edaphic suitability*

As a medium in which roots grow and as a reservoir for water and nutrients upon which plants continuously draw, soil represents an important natural resource and valuable economic asset requiring protection and improvement through good land use husbandry.

The adequate exploitation of the climatic potential or sustained maintenance of productivity largely depends on soil fertility and using soil on an ecologically sound basis. Soil fertility is concerned with the ability of soil to supply nutrients and water as well as the ability of soil to respond to application of production treatments. The fertility of a soil is

TABLE 4.16
Quartiles of slope classes

Slope class		Gentlest	Lower	Upper	Steepest
Symbol	%	Q1	Q2	Q3	Q4
A	0 - 2	0	1	1	2
AB	0 - 5	0	2	4	5
B	2 - 5	2	3	4	5
BC	2 - 8	2	4	6	8
C	5 - 8	5	6	7	8
BCD	2 - 16	2	6	11	16
CD	5 - 16	5	9	12	16
D	8 - 16	8	11	13	16
DE	8 - 30	8	16	22	30
E	16 - 30	16	21	25	30
EF	16 - 56	16	30	42	56
F	30 - 56	30	39	47	56

determined by both its physical and chemical properties whose understanding is essential to the effective utilization of the climatic resources.

In order to assess soil suitability for pasture production, the soil requirements of pasture species must be determined. Further, these requirements must be understood within the context of limitations imposed by landform and other features (e.g. soil phases, stoniness) which do not form part of soil composition but have a significant influence on the use that can be made of the soil.

Basic soil requirements for pasture species relate to the following internal soil properties:

(i)   the soil temperature regime, as a function of the heat balance of soils as related to annual or seasonal and/or daily temperature fluctuations;

(ii)   the soil moisture regime, as a function of the water balance of soils as related to the soil's capacity to store, retain, transport and release moisture for plant growth, and/or to the soil's permeability and drainage characteristics;

(iii)   the soil aeration regime, as a function of the soil air balance as related to its capacity to supply and transport oxygen to the root zone and to remove carbon dioxide;

(iv)   the natural soil fertility regime, as related to the soil's capacity to store, retain and release plant nutrients in such kinds and proportions as required by pasture species during growth;

(v)   the effective soil depth available for root development and physical support of plants;

(vi)   soil texture and stoniness at the surface and within the whole depth of soil required for normal pasture development;

(vii)   the absence of soil salinity and of specific toxic substance or ions deleterious to plant growth; and

TABLE 4.17
Relations between basic soil requirements for pasture species and soil characteristics

Basic soil requirements	Soil characteristics (soil factors)
Moisture availability[1]	- Effective soil depth - Available soil moisture holding capacity - Drainage
Nutrient availability	- Nutrient availability - Soil reaction
Oxygen availability[2]	- Soil permeability, Drainage
Foothold for roots	- Effective soil depth
Salinity	- Soil salinity
Toxicity	- Soil reaction[3]
Accessibility and trafficability (workability)	- Topsoil consistency and bearing capacity
Soil tilth for species establishment	- Topsoil consistency and bearing capacity

[1] Moisture availability is influenced by climatic factors.
[2] Oxygen availability is influenced by inundation and flooding characteristics.
[3] Chemical properties of soil parent material may also be involved in some cases.

(viii)   other specific properties, e.g. soil tilth as required for germination and early plant growth.

From the basic soil requirements for pasture species, a number of responses related to soil characteristics have been derived. The correlation between the basic soil requirements listed above and soil characteristics that can be used as soil factors to rate pasture and fodder crop performance is given in Table 4.17.

As explained earlier, the soil units (Table 4.12) have been defined in terms of measurable and observable properties of the soil itself, and specific clusters of such properties are combined into "diagnostic horizons" and "diagnostic properties", which are used in the definition of the soil units.

The diagnostic horizons have been used as defined in the FAO-Unesco Soil Map Legend. Diagnostic properties however have been narrowed down in case of ferric properties and widened in case of vertic properties. In Table 4.18 for each soil unit diagnostic horizons and properties of the soil units are summarized. For the ease of interpretation of Table 4.18, these characteristics are summarized below.

Histic H horizon: Surface layer of organic material more than 20 cm thick.

Mollic A horizon: Surface horizon with dark colour, medium to high humus content, high base saturation.

Umbric A horizon: Surface horizon with dark colour, medium to high humus content, low base saturation.

Ochric A horizon:	Surface horizon with light colour, low humus content.
Argillic B horizon:	Subsoil horizon with accumulation of illuvial clay.
Natric B horizon:	Subsoil horizon with accumulation of illuvial clay and high exchangeable sodium.
Cambic B horizon:	Subsoil horizon with a structure and/or colour different from overlying and underlying horizons.
Spodic B horizon:	Subsoil horizon with accumulation of iron and/or humus.
Oxic B horizon:	Subsoil with residual accumulation of sesquioxides and low CEC.
Calcic horizon:	Horizon of accumulation of calcium carbonate.
Gypsic horizon:	Horizon of accumulation of calcium sulphate.
Sulphuric horizon:	Horizon with strong acidity and prominent mottling.
Albic E horizon:	Eluvial horizon from which clay and free iron oxide have been removed, light colour.
Calcareous material:	Calcium carbonate present at least between 20 and 50 cm from the surface.
CEC high or very high:	Exchange complex dominated by allophane or montmorillonite.
CEC low:	Exchange complex dominated by kaolinite (CEC less than 24 meq/100 g clay).
CEC very low:	Less than 1.5 meq/100 g clay.
Cracking clays:	Formation of deep and wide cracks upon drying.
Plinthite:	Mottled subsoil layer which irreversibly hardens upon exposure to repeated wetting and drying.
High salinity:	Electrical conductivity (EC) higher than 15 mmhos/cm.
Moderate salinity:	Electrical conductivity (EC) between 4 and 15 mmhos/cm.
High alkalinity:	Saturation with exchangeable sodium of more than 15%.
Moderate alkalinity:	Saturation with exchangeable sodium of 6 to 15%.
Indurated subsoil:	Subsoil layer with firm or hard consistence, but can still be penetrated by spade or auger.

Cemented hardpan:	Extremely hard continuous subsoil layer which cannot be penetrated by spade or auger.
Coarse texture:	Less than 18% clay and more than 65% sand.
Heavy texture:	More than 35% clay.
Abrupt textural change:	Considerable increase in clay content within a very short vertical distance.
Tonguing:	Deep and irregular penetration of an albic E horizon into an argillic B horizon.

The edaphic suitability classification is input-specific and based on:

(i)   matching the soil requirements of pasture and fodder species with the soil conditions of the soil units described in the soil inventory (soil unit evaluation), and
(ii) modification of the soil unit evaluation by limitation imposed by texture, phase and slope conditions.

The soil unit evaluation for pasture and fodder production is expressed in terms of ratings based on how far the soil conditions of a soil unit meet the growth and production requirements under a specified level of inputs. The appraisal is effected in five basic classes for pasture and fodder grasses and legumes as a group, i.e. very suitable (S1), suitable (S2), moderately suitable (S3), marginally suitable (S4), and not suitable (N).

A rating of S1 indicates that the soil conditions are optimal, and that suppression of potential yields (if any) is assumed to be nil or slight. A rating of S2 indicates that there are slight to moderate soil constraints and there would be a suppression of potential yields of the order of 25%. A rating of S3 indicates that there are with moderate to severe soil constraints and there would a suppression of potential yields of the order of 50%. A rating of S4 indicates that there are severe soil constraints and there would be a suppression of potential yields of the order of 75%. A rating of N indicates that soil conditions are not suitable for production.

The soil unit ratings are presented in Table 4.19 and apply as indicated provided there are no additional limitations imposed by soil texture, phase and stoniness. Modifications are required where such limitations are present.

In the case of soil texture, soil unit ratings remain unchanged if the soil is an albic, cambic, ferralic, calcaro-cambic or luvic Arenosol (Q, Qa, Qc, Qf, Qkc, Ql) or a vitric Andosol (Tv), or where textures are medium (fine sandy loam, sandy loam, loam, sandy clay loam, clay loam, silty clay loam, silt), or fine (sandy clay, silty clay, peaty clay, clay). In all other cases (i.e. with coarse textures: sand, loamy coarse sand, fine sand, loamy fine sand, loamy sand) the soil unit rating is one class (25%) lower.

Limitations imposed by phase and stoniness are rated using the five basic classes already described. The phase ratings are presented in Table 4.20, and the stoniness ratings in Table 4.21.

TABLE 4.18
Diagnostic horizons and properties of soil units

	A	Ac	Ag	Ah	Aic	Aif	Aio	Ao	Ap	Ath	B	Bc	Bd	Be	Bf	Bg	Bh	Bk	Bnc	Btc	Bte	Bv	C	Ch	Ck
Histic H horizon																									
Mollic A horizon																							x	x	x
Umbric A horizon			(x	x						x						(x	x								
Ochric A horizon	x	x	(x		x	x	x	x	x		x	x	x	x	x	(x		x	x	x	x	x	x		
Argillic B horizon	x	x	x	x	x	x	x	x	x	x	x														
Natric B horizon																									
Cambic B horizon												x	x	x	x	x	x	x	x	x	x	x	x	x	x
Spodic B horizon																									
Oxic B horizon																									
Calcic horizon																		x							x
Gypsic horizon																									
Sulfuric horizon																									
Albic E horizon (nat.)																									
Calcareous material																		x						x	x
CaCO₃ > 5% (topsoil)																							x		
CEC high/very high																									
CEC low (<24 meq)					x		x								x										
CEC very low (<1.5 meq)						x																			
Base sat. >50%, (pH>5.5)												x	x	x		x		x	x	x	x	x	x	x	x
Base sat. <50%, (pH<5.5)	x	x	x	x	x	x	x	x	x	x	x		x					x							
Cracking clay																						x			
Depth <25 cm																									
Depth 25-50 cm																									
Drainage very poor/poor			x																						
Drainage imp./moderate									x							x									
Drainage excessive																									
Plinthite									x																
Salinity high																									
Salinity moderate																									
Alkalinity high																									
Alkalinity moderate																									
Indurated subsoil																									
Cemented hardpan																									
Iron concretions						x									x										
Texture coarse																									
Texture heavy												x							x	x	x				
Abrupt textural change																									
Tonguing																									
Reddish colour		x			x							x							x	x					
Yellowish colour																									
Nat. fertility high												x				x		x	x		x	x	x	x	x
Nat. fertility moderate	x	x		x	x		x	x		x		x	x				x		x	x					
Nat. fertility low			x			x			x						x										

	A	Ac	Ag	Ah	Aic	Aif	Aio	Ao	Ap	Ath	B	Bc	Bd	Be	Bf	Bg	Bh	Bk	Bnc	Btc	Bte	Bv	C	Ch	Ck

(indicates mutually exclusive horizons

TABLE 4.18 (Continued)

	E	Ec	Eo	F	Fa	Fh	Fnh	Fnr	Fo	Fr	Fx	G	Gc	Gd	Ge	Gh	Gm	Gv	H	Hg	Hh	Hnl	Hol	Hrl	Hth
Histic H horizon																(x	(x								
Mollic A horizon	x	x	x														(x		x	x	x	x	x	x	x
Umbric A horizon						x	x									(x									
Ochric A horizon					x	x		x	x	x	x	x	x	x	x			x							
Argillic B horizon																				x					
Natric B horizon																									
Cambic B horizon													x	x	x	x	x	x	x	x		x			x
Spodic B horizon																									
Oxic B horizon					x	x	x	x	x	x	x	x													
Calcic horizon														x											
Gypsic horizon																									
Sulferic horizon																									
Albic E horizon (nat.)																									
Calcareous material	x	x	x								x														
CaCO₃ > 5% (topsoil)		x																							
CEC high/very high																									
CEC low (<24 meq)					x		x	x	x	x	x	x													
CEC very low (<1.5 meq)						x																			
Base sat. >50%, (pH>5.5)													x	x		x		x							
Base sat. <50%, (pH<5.5)					x			x			x					x	x	x							
Cracking clay																		x							
Depth <25 cm																									
Depth 25-50 cm	x	x	x																						
Drainage very poor/poor													x	x	x	x	x	x	x		x				
Drainage imp./moderate																									
Drainage excessive																									
Plinthite																									
Salinity high																									
Salinity moderate																									
Alkalinity high																									
Alkalinity moderate																									
Indurated subsoil																									
Cemented hardpan																									
Iron concretions																									
Texture coarse											x														
Texture heavy							x	x																	
Abrupt textural change																									
Tonguing																									
Reddish colour									x															x	
Yellowish colour									x																
Nat. fertility high	x	x	x										x	x	x	x	x	x	x	x	x	x	x	x	x
Nat. fertility moderate						x	x	x		x				x											
Nat. fertility low					x	x			x		x														

| | E | Ec | Eo | F | Fa | Fh | Fnh | Fnr | Fo | Fr | Fx | G | Gc | Gd | Ge | Gh | Gm | Gv | H | Hg | Hh | Hnl | Hol | Hrl | Hth |

(indicates mutually exclusive horizons

TABLE 4.18 (Continued)

	Htl	Hvl	I	Ir	J	Jc	Je	Jt	K	Kh	L	La	Lc	Lf	Lg	Lic	Lif	Lio	Lk	Lnc	Lnf	Lo	Lv	M	Mo
Histic H horizon																									
Mollic A horizon	x	x							x	x														x	x
Umbric A horizon				(x																					
Ochric A horizon						x	x	x	(x		x	x	x	x	x	x	x	x	x	x	x	x		x	x
Argillic B horizon	x	x									x	x	x	x	x	x	x	x	x	x	x	x	x	x	x
Natric B horizon																									
Cambic B horizon									x	x															
Spodic B horizon																									
Oxic B horizon																									
Calcic horizon						x													x						
Gypsic horizon																									
Sulferic horizon								x																	
Albic E horizon (nat.)															x										
Calcareous material									x	x															
CaCO₃ > 5% (topsoil)																									
CEC high/very high																									
CEC low (<24 meq)																x			x						
CEC very low (<1.5 meq)														x					x						
Base sat. >50%, (pH>5.5)						x	x	x		x	x	x	x	x	x	x	x	x	x	x	x	x	x		
Base sat. <50%, (pH<5.5)																									
Cracking clay	x																						x		
Depth <25 cm			x																						
Depth 25-50 cm				x																					
Drainage very poor/poor															x										
Drainage imp./moderate																									
Drainage excessive																									
Plinthite																									
Salinity high																									
Salinity moderate																									
Alkalinity high																									
Alkalinity moderate																									
Indurated subsoil																									
Cemented hardpan																									
Iron concretions					x									x			x			x					
Texture coarse																									
Texture heavy																							x		
Abrupt textural change																									
Tonguing																									
Reddish colour														x		x			x						
Yellowish colour																									
Nat. fertility high	x	x			x	x	x		x	x	x								x					x	x
Nat. fertility moderate														x		x	x	x			x			x	x
Nat. fertility low											x		x		x							x			

| | Htl | Hvl | I | Ir | J | Jc | Je | Jt | K | Kh | L | La | Lc | Lf | Lg | Lic | Lif | Lio | Lk | Lnc | Lnf | Lo | Lv | M | Mo |

(indicates mutually exclusive horizons

TABLE 4.18 (Continued)

	Mvo	M	Md	Me	Mh	Mm	Mth	Mve	Mvm	O	Od	Q	Qa	Qc	Qf	Qk	Ql	R	Rc	Rd	Re	Rtc	S	Sg	Slo
Histic H horizon										x	x														
Mollic A horizon	x					x			x																
Umbric A horizon					x		x																		
Ochric A horizon			x	x	x		x				x	x	x	x	x	x	x	x	x	x	x	x	x		x
Argillic B horizon	x	x	x	x	x	x	x	x	x							x									
Natric B horizon																							x	x	x
Cambic B horizon													x	x											
Spodic B horizon																									
Oxic B horizon																									
Calcic horizon																x									
Gypsic horizon																									
Sulfuric horizon																									
Albic E horizon (nat.)														x											
Calcareous material														x			x			x					
CaCO₃ > 5% (topsoil)																									
CEC high/very high																									
CEC low (<24 meq)														x											
CEC very low (<1.5 meq)																									
Base sat. >50%, (pH>5.5)		x		x		x	x	x											x	x		x	x		
Base sat. <50%, (pH<5.5)			x		x	x				x										x					
Cracking clay	x						x	x																	
Depth <25 cm																									
Depth 25-50 cm																									
Drainage very poor/poor																								x	
Drainage imp./moderate																									
Drainage excessive											x	x	x	x	x	x									
Plinthite																									
Salinity high																									
Salinity moderate																									
Alkalinity high																								x	x
Alkalinity moderate																									
Indurated subsoil																									
Cemented hardpan																									
Iron concretions														x											
Texture coarse											x	x	x	x	x	x									
Texture heavy	x						x	x																	
Abrupt textural change																									
Tonguing																									
Reddish colour																									
Yellowish colour																									
Nat. fertility high			x	x		x	x	x											x	x		x	x		
Nat. fertility moderate	x		x		x	x														x					
Nat. fertility low										x	x	x	x	x	x	x									

	Mvo	M	Md	Me	Mh	Mm	Mth	Mve	Mvm	O	Od	Q	Qa	Qc	Qf	Qk	Ql	R	Rc	Rd	Re	Rtc	S	Sg	Slo

TABLE 4.18 (Continued)

	Sa	So	T	Th	Ta	Tv	U	V	Vc	Vp	W	Wd	We	Wh	Ws	Wve	X	Xh	Xk	Xy	Z	Zg	Zo	Zt
Histic H horizon																								
Mollic A horizon	x				x									(x										
Umbric A horizon				x			x																	
Ochric A horizon		x	x		x						x	x	(x	x	x	x	x	x	x	x	x	x	x	x
Argillic B horizon											x	x	x	x	x	x								
Natric B horizon	x	x																						
Cambic B horizon			x	x	x	x											x	x			x	x	x	x
Spodic B horizon																								
Oxic B horizon																								
Calcic horizon																				x				
Gypsic horizon																								
Sulfuric horizon																								
Albic E horizon (nat.)								x	x	x	x	x	x											
Calcareous material																								
CaCO₃ > 5% (topsoil)																								
CEC high/very high		x	x	x		x	x	x																
CEC low (<24 meq)																								
CEC very low (<1.5 meq)																								
Base sat. >50%, (pH>5.5)	x				x						x		x		x	x			x	x				
Base sat. <50%, (pH<5.5)		x											x	x										
Cracking clay				x	x	x									x									x
Depth <25 cm																								
Depth 25-50 cm							x																	
Drainage very poor/poor																				x				
Drainage imp./moderate											x	x	x	x	x	x								
Drainage excessive																								
Plinthite																								
Salinity high																					x	x	x	x
Salinity moderate															x									
Alkalinity high	x	x																						
Alkalinity moderate																								
Indurated subsoil																								
Cemented hardpan																								
Iron concretions																								
Texture coarse						x																		
Texture heavy				x	x	x																		x
Abrupt textural change								x	x	x	x	x	x											
Tonguing																								
Reddish colour																								
Yellowish colour																								
Nat. fertility high					x			x	x	x							x	x	x					
Nat. fertility moderate		x	x								x		x		x									
Nat. fertility low						x	x						x	x										

	Sa	So	T	Th	Ta	Tv	U	V	Vc	Vp	W	Wd	We	Wh	Ws	Wve	X	Xh	Xk	Xy	Z	Zg	Zo	Zt

(indicates mutually exclusive horizons

TABLE 4.19
Soil unit ratings for pasture at high, intermediate and low levels of inputs

Soil unit[1]	Inputs level			Soil unit	Inputs level			Soil uit	Inputs level		
	High	Int.	Low		High	Int.	Low		High	Int.	Low
A	S1	S2	S3	H	S1	S1	S1	O	S4	S4	S4
Ac	S1	S2	S3	Hg	S3	S3	S3	Od	S4	S4	S4
Ag	S4	S4	S4	Hh	S1	S1	S1	Q	S1	S2	S3
Aic	S1	S2	S3	Hnl	S1	S1	S1	Qa	S3	S3	S3
Aif	S1	S2	S3	Hol	S1	S1	S1	Qc	S1	S2	S3
Aio	S1	S2	S3	Hrl	S1	S1	S1	Qf	S2	S2	S3
Ao	S1	S2	S3	Hth	S1	S1	S1	Qkc	S1	S2	S3
Ap	S3	S4	S4	Htl	S1	S1	S1	Ql	S1	S2	S3
Ath	S1	S2	S3	Hvl	S1	S1	S1	R	S2	S2	S2
B	S1	S1	S1	I	N	S4	S4	Rc	S2	S2	S2
Bc	S1	S1	S1	Ir	N	S4	S4	Rd	S2	S2	S2
Bd	S1	S2	S3	J	S1	S1	S1	Re	S2	S2	S2
Be	S1	S1	S1	Je	S1	S1	S1	Rtc	S2	S2	S2
Bf	S2	S2	S3	Jt	S4	S4	S4	S	S4	S4	S4
Bg	S1	S1	S1	K	S1	S1	S1	Sg	S4	S4	S4
Bh	S1	S1	S1	Kh	S1	S1	S1	Slo	S4	S4	S4
Bk	S1	S1	S1	L	S1	S1	S1	Sm	S4	S4	S4
Bnc	S1	S1	S1	La	S1	S2	S3	So	S4	S4	S4
Btc	S1	S1	S1	Lc	S1	S1	S1	T	S1	S1	S1
Bte	S1	S1	S1	Lf	S2	S2	S3	Th	S1	S1	S1
Bv	S1	S1	S2	Lg	S3	S3	S3	Tm	S1	S1	S1
Ch	S1	S1	S1	Lic	S1	S1	S2	Tv	S4	S4	S4
Ck	S1	S1	S1	Lif	S1	S1	S3	U	S4	S4	S4
Ec	S3	S3	S3	Lio	S1	S1	S1	V	S1	S2	S3
Eo	S3	S3	S3	Lk	S1	S1	S1	Vc	S1	S2	S3
F	S1	S2	S3	Lnc	S1	S1	S1	Vp	S1	S2	S3
Fa	S3	S4	S4	Lnf	S2	S2	S3	W	S2	S2	S3
Fh	S1	S2	S3	Lo	S1	S1	S1	Wd	S3	S3	S3
Fnh	S1	S2	S3	Lv	S1	S1	S2	We	S2	S2	S3
Fnr	S1	S2	S3	Mo	S1	S1	S1	Wh	S2	S2	S3
Fo	S3	S3	S3	Mvo	S1	S1	S2	Ws	S4	S4	S4
Fr	S1	S2	S3	N	S1	S1	S1	Wve	S2	S3	S4
Fx	S1	S3	S3	Nd	S1	S1	S3	X	S2	S2	S2
G/Ge	S4	S4	S4	Ne	S1	S1	S1	Xh	S2	S2	S2
Gc	S4	S4	S4	Nh	S1	S1	S2	Xk	S2	S2	S2
Gd	S4	S4	S4	Nm	S1	S1	S1	Z	S4	S4	S4
Gh	S4	S4	S4	Nth	S1	S1	S2	Zg	S4	S4	S4
Gm	S4	S4	S4	Nve	S1	S1	S2	Zo	S4	S4	S4
Gv	S4	S4	S4	Nvm	S1	S1	S2	Zt	S4	S4	S4

[1] See Table 4.12 for soil unit names

4.2.7 *Slope limitations and soil erosion*

Limitations imposed by slope are taken into account in three steps. Step one defines the slopes which are permissible for pastures production, and as a model variable this is defined as slopes less than 45%.

Step two involves the computation of potential topsoil loss which is estimated, by inputs level, through a modified Universal Soil Loss Equation (Wischmeier and Smith 1978).

TABLE 4.20
Soil phase ratings for pasture at high, intermediate and low levels of inputs

Phase[1]	Inputs level			Phase	Inputs level			Phase	Inputs level		
	High	Int.	Low		High	Int.	Low		High	Int.	Low
R	N	S3	S3	R/B	N	S4	S4	R/B/AO	N	N	N
B	N	S3	S3	R/S	N	S4	S4	R/P/S	N	N	N
BM	N	N	N	B/S	N	S4	S4	B/S/A	N	N	N
S	N	S3	S3	BM/AO	N	N	N	BM/S/AO	N	N	N
SM	N	N	N	S/R	N	S4	S4	P/R/B	N	N	N
G	S2	S2	S2	S/B	N	S4	S4	P/R/S	N	N	N
GM	N	S	N	S/K	N	S4	S4	P/B/S	N	N	N
P	N	S3	S3	S/AO	N	N	N	P/B/A	N	N	N
PP	S4	S3	S3	SM/O	N	N	N	P/BM/AO	N	N	N
K	N	S3	S3	SM/AO	N	N	N	P/S/R	N	N	N
KK	S4	S2	S2	P/R	N	N	N	P/S/A	N	N	N
C	N	S4	S3	P/B	N	N	N	P/S/AO	N	N	N
CC	S4	S3	S2	P/BM	N	N	N	P/SM/AO	N	N	N
M	S4	S2	S2	P/S	N	N	N	P/GM/S	N	N	N
MM	S2	S2	S2	P/O	N	N	N				
A	S2	S2	S2	P/AO	N	N	N				
O	S2	S2	S2	PP/R	N	N	N				
AO	S4	S4	S4	PP/S	N	N	N				
F	S2	S2	S2	K/S	N	S4	S4				
				K/AO	N	N	N				
				KK/A	N	S3	S3				
				KK/O	N	S3	S3				
				N/R	N	S4	S3				
				N/M	N	S4	S3				
				A/F	S3	S3	S3				
				O/F	S3	S3	S3				

[1] See Table 4.14 for soil phase names

Step three relates the estimated topsoil losses to yield losses through a set of equations given in Table 4.22, taking into account soil susceptibility, and level of inputs. The reduced impact at intermediate and high inputs is due to the compensating effect of fertilizer applications at their normal rates of use.

Steps two and three are described in detail in Technical Annex 2, and Mitchell (1986). Table 4.23 shows the soil units ranked in three classes according to their susceptibility to yield losses in relation to loss of topsoil, on the basis of organic matter content, soil depth and on the presence of other unfavourable subsoil conditions.

TABLE 4.21
Stoniness ratings for pasture at high, intermediate and low levels of inputs

Stoniness type	Inputs level		
	High	Int.	Low
Gravelly	S3	S2	S2
Very gravelly	N	S4	S4
Stony	N	S3	S3
Bouldery	N	S3	S3
Stony/bouldery	N	S4	S4
Bouldery/stony	N	S4	S4

In estimating yield losses from equations in Table 4.22 regeneration capacity of soils is taken into account in calculating net loss of top soil. Regeneration capacities of topsoils by thermal and moisture regimes are given in Table 4.24.

4.2.8 *Land suitability*

All three assessments: the climatic suitability, the edaphic suitability and the soil erosion hazard, are required to determine the ecological land suitability for grassland/pasture production of each climate-soil unit of the land resources inventory. In essence the land suitability assessment takes account of all the inventoried attributes of land and compares them with the requirements of pasture species, to give an easy to understand picture of the suitability of land for grassland/pasture production.

The results of the land suitability assessment are presented in five basic suitability classes, each linked to attainable yields for the three levels of inputs considered. For each level of inputs, the land suitability classes are: very suitable (VS) - 80% or more of the maximum attainable yield; suitable (S) - 60% to less than 80% of the maximum attainable yield; moderately suitable (MS) - 40% to less than 60% of the maximum attainable yields; marginally suitable (mS) - 20% to less than 40%; and not suitable (NS) - less than 20%.

Table 4.22
Relationships between topsoil loss and yield loss

Soil susceptibility ranking	Levels of inputs	Equation
Least susceptible	Low	Y = 1.0 X
	Intermediate	Y = 0.6 X
	High	Y = 0.2 X
Intermediate susceptible	Low	Y = 2.0 X
	Intermediate	Y = 1.2 X
	High	Y = 0.4 X
Most susceptible	Low	Y = 7.0 X
	Intermediate	Y = 5.0 X
	High	Y = 3.0 X

Y = productivity loss in percent
X = soil loss in cm

Table 4.23
Ranking of soils (Kenya Soil Survey) according to their susceptibility to productivity loss per unit of topsoil loss

Least susceptible	Most susceptibile	Intermediate susceptible
Chernozems	Acrisols, except	Arenosols
Fluvisols	Humic Acrisols	Cambisols, except
Histosols	Ferralic Cambisols	Ferralic Cambisols
Humic Andosols	Ferralsols, except	Gleysols
Mollic Andosols	Humic Ferralsols	Greyzems
Vertisols	Ironstone soils	Humic Acrisols
	Lithosols	Humic Ferralsols
	Planosols	Kastanozems
	Rendzinas	Luvisols
	Solonchaks	Nitisols
	Solonetz	Phaeozems
		Regosols
		Vitric Andosols
		Xerosols
		Yermosols

TABLE 4.24
Regeneration capacity of topsoil (mm/year) by length of growing period (LGP) and thermal zone (derived from Hammer (1981)

LGP (days)	Thermal zone								
	T1	T2	T3	T4	T5	T6	T7	T8	T9
<75	0.5	0.5	0.5	0.5	0.5	0.25	0.25	0.25	0.25
75-	1.0	1.0	1.0	0.5	0.5	0.25	0.25	0.25	0.25
179	1.5	1.5	1.5	0.75	0.75	0.5	0.5	0.5	0.5
180-	2.0	2.0	2.0	1.0	1.0	0.5	0.5	0.5	0.5
269									
>270									

Land suitability assessment is achieved by applying the programme illustrated in Figure 4.3.

Firstly, the temperature requirements of the grass and legume species with regard to photosynthesis and phenology are compared with prevailing temperature conditions of each thermal zone. If they do not accord, all the growing period zones in that thermal zone are classified as not suitable. If the temperature conditions of a thermal zone do partially or fully accord with the crop thermal requirements, all growing period zones in that thermal zone are considered for further suitability assessment according to the thermal zone rating.

This further assessment comprises application of length of growing period suitability to the computed areas of the various growing period zones by LGP-Pattern zone. Thus if the thermal zone rating of a particular growing period zone is S1, then potential yield biomass value for the growing period zone is not modified. If the thermal zone rating of the growing period zone is S3, then the potential yield biomass value for the computed extents of the period zone is decreased by 50%. The thermal and moisture suitability assessments are described in Section 4.2.3.

The length of growing period suitability and yields are applied according to the LGP-Pattern make up of LGP zone. All pasture species and yields are matched to the individual component length of growing period, i.e. L1, $L2^1$, $L2^2$ $L3^1$, $L3^2$, $L3^3$, $L4^1$, $L4^2$, $L4^3$ and $L4^4$. The LGP-Pattern evaluation for each crop is achieved by taking into account the constituent component lengths of each LGP-Pattern, thus providing a profile of variability in potential yields over time (e.g. average yield, maximum yield, minimum yield).

The next step is an appraisal of the soil units present in each growing period zone. The rating of soil units, for pasture and level of inputs under consideration, is applied to the computed area of the growing period zone occupied by each soil unit. The appraisal, undertaken on the basis of the soil ratings as described in Section 4.2.6, leads to appropriate modifications of the climatic suitability assessment and the attainable total and consumable biomass. Subsequently, the ratings for the different soil textures, phases and stoniness are applied consecutively.

Finally, limitations imposed by slope are taken into account to arrive at the final land suitability appraisal for pasture, for the level of inputs under consideration.

The five classes of land suitabilities are related to attainable yield as a percentage of the maximum attainable yield under the optimum climatic, edaphic and landform conditions. Consequently the results provide an assessment of pasture production potentials of each land unit, which in turn can be aggregated for any given area in Kenya.

Generalized results of land suitability assessment for pasture production at intermediate level of inputs are presented in Figure 4.4, and in Technical Annex 1.8. It should be noted that the generalized results presented include a subdivision of the not suitable class (zero to less than 20% of the maximum attainable yield) into two classes (1) very marginally suitable (more than zero to less than 20% of maximum attainable yield) and (2) not suitable (zero yield).

38

A case study of Kenya. Technical Annex 5

FIGURE 4.3
Schematic presentation of the land suitability assessment programme for pasture production

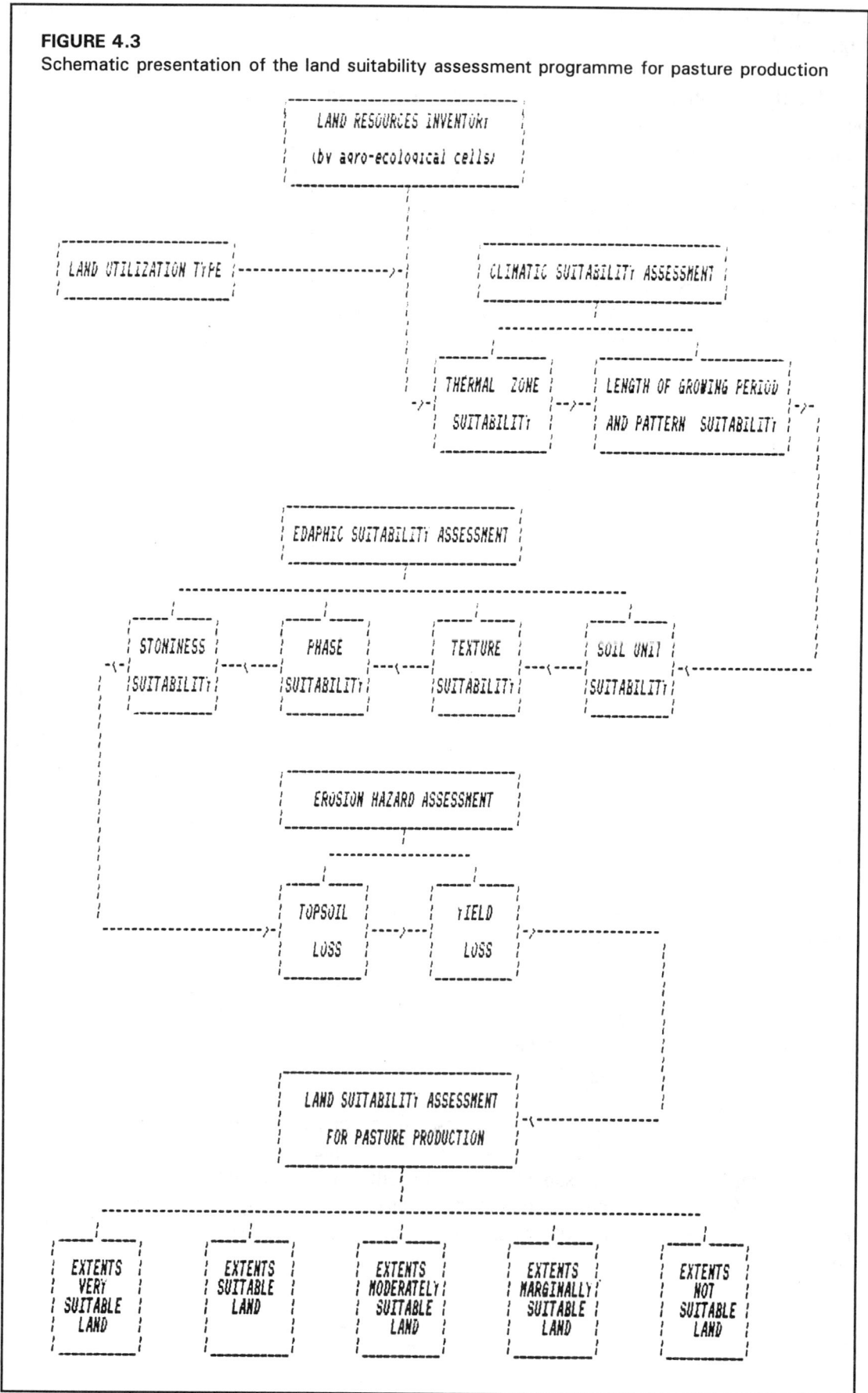

FIGURE 4.4
Generalized land suitability for rainfed pasture production at intermediate level of inputs

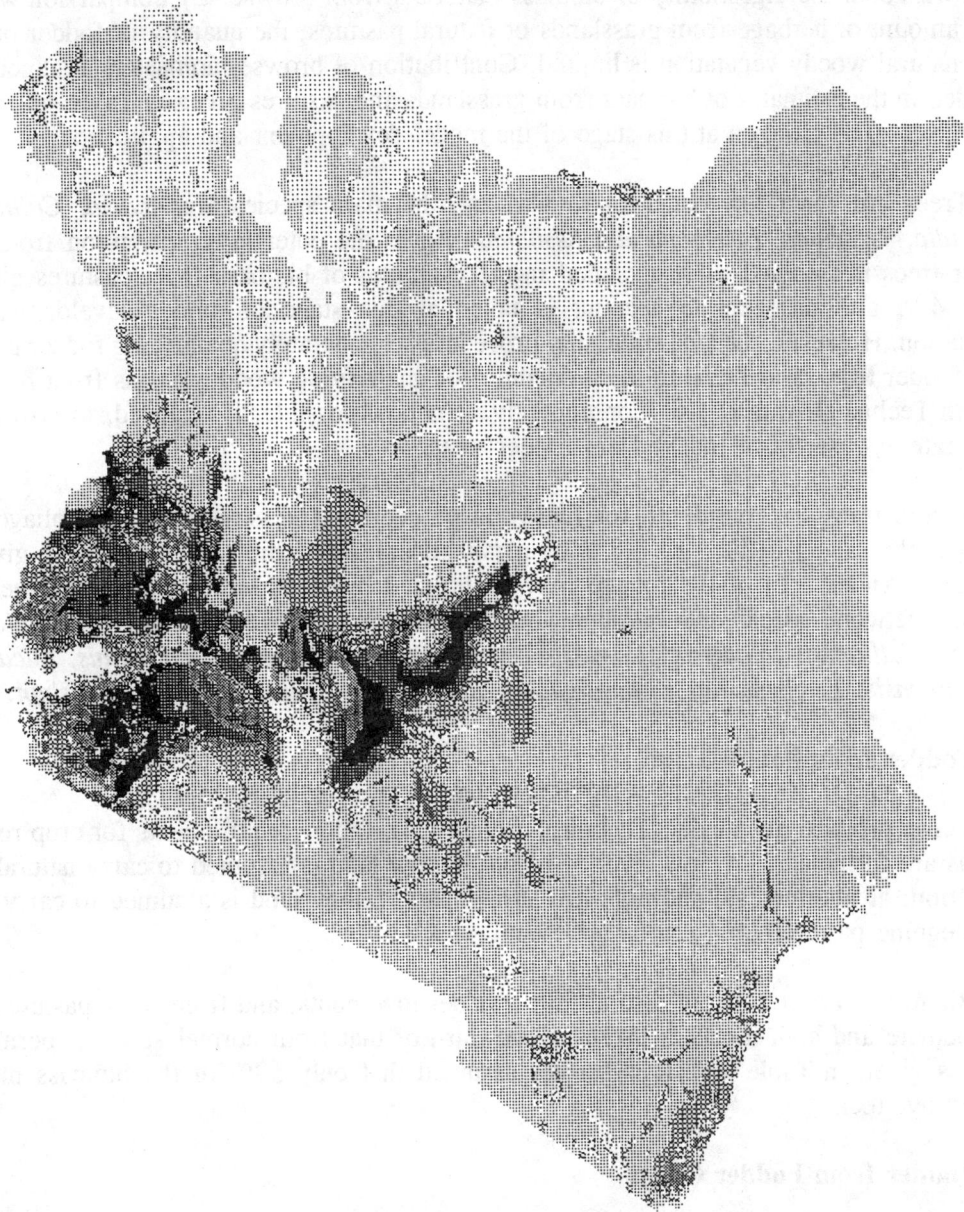

■ Very suitable	(80-100% MAY)
▓ Suitable	(60- 80% MAY)
▒ Moderately suitable	(40- 60% MAY)
▒ Marginally suitable	(20- 40% MAY)
░ Very marginally suitable	(1- 20% MAY)
░ Not suitable	(0% MAY)

MAY - maximum attainable yield

4.3 Fodder from Browse, Fodder Trees and Fuelwood Trees

In the low rainfall areas (LGP < 120 days), natural woody vegetation including leguminous shrubs and trees can be important in the nutrition of domestic stock. However, relatively little is known about the digestibility of biomass materials from browse. By comparison with the large amount of herbage from grasslands or natural pastures, the quantity of fodder biomass from natural woody vegetation is limited. Contribution of browse biomass is assumed to be included in the estimates of biomass from grasslands and pastures given in Table 4.9, and no separate account is taken at this stage of the model development and application.

Trees are sown for fodder in Kenya, and the main species are *Acacia, Calliandra, Gliricidia, Grevillea, Leucaena* and *Sesbania.* Again the potential contribution from sown fodder trees is assumed to be included in the estimates of biomass from pastures given in Table 4.9, and no seperate account is taken at this stage of model development and application. However, the land suitability procedure for seperately quantifying fodder biomass from fodder trees is identical to the procedure for quantifying wood biomass from fuelwood trees in Technical Annex 1.6. Consequently, it is now possible, if required, to provide for a separate assessment of fodder from fodder trees.

Where trees are considered for fuelwood production and carry palatable foliage, it is assumed that about 10% (i.e. 3.3% of mean annual wood biomass increments given in Technical Annex 1.6) of the foliage may be utilized by stock without affecting fuelwood yields. Fuelwood species that can contribute fodder are: *Acacia gerrardia, A. nilotica, A. senegal, Calliandra calothyrus, Casuarina equisetifolia, Conocarpus lancifolius, Eucalyptus camaldulensis, E. citridoria, E. tereticornis, Parkinsonia aculeata, Sesbania sesban.*

4.4 Fodder from Fallow Land

In the crop productivity model (Technical Annex 1.4), fallow requirements for crop rotation options are formulated. At low level of inputs, fallow land is assumed to carry natural bush vegetation; at intermediate and high levels of inputs, fallow land is assumed to carry sown grass-legume pasture.

Biomass production from natural fallow under low inputs, and from sown pasture under intermediate and high inputs is taken as one-third of that from normal sown or permanent pastures given in Table 4.9. It is further assumed that only 50% of the biomass may be utilized by stock.

4.5 Fodder from Fodder Crops

Fodder grasses, legumes and cereals are grown for fodder production in Kenya. Main fodder grasses are *Pennisetum purpureum* (Napier or Bana grass), *Setaria splendida* (Giant setaria), *Sorghum sudanense* (Sudan grass) and *Tripsacum laxacum* (Guatemala grass). Main fodder legume species are *Centrosema pubescens, Lablab purpureus* or *Lablab niger* (Hyacinth bean), *Macroptilium atropurpureum* (Siratro), *Vigna* spp. and *Stylosanthes* spp. Main fodder cereals are maize, oat, pearl millet and sorghum.

A separate assessment of biomass potential from fodder grasses, legumes and cereals is possible according to the land suitability methodology described in Technical Annex 3. However, at this stage of model development and application, the range of biomass potentials from pastures given in Table 4.9, are found to adequately cover the biological potentials of fodder crops.

4.6 Crop Residues, By-products and Primary Products

In areas with more than 120 days growing period, crop residues are an important source of fodder particularly for the low and intermediate technology livestock systems. Important residues are the haulms of groundnut, cowpea and other grain legumes, and the staves (stalks) of sorghum, maize and millet, and straw from rice, wheat, barley and oat. Quantities of residues that may be available have been estimated by applying the residue factor (Cr) and the corresponding utilization coefficients (Cru) and (Cbu) to crop yields (Table 4.25).

By-products, defined as edible materials remaining after a crop has been processed, are bran and germ meal from cereal milling; molasses and bagasse from sugar milling; and cakes (cotton, soybean, groundnut) from oilseeds. Quantities of crop by-products that may be available have been estimated by applying the by-product factor (Cb) and the corresponding utilization coefficients (Cbu) onto crop yields (Table 4.25).

TABLE 4.25
Crop residue (Cr) and by-product (Cb) factors

Crop	Cr	Cru	Cb	Cbu
1 Millet	5.0	0.2	0.08	0.9
2 Sorghum	5.0	0.2	0.08	0.8
3 Maize	3.0	0.3	0.20	0.9
4 Bunded rice	1.3	0.4	0.08	0.9
5 Upland rice	3.0	0.4	0.08	0.9
6 Wheat	2.0	0.4	0.20	0.9
7 Barley	1.5	0.3	0.20	0.9
8 Oat	1.5	0.3	0.20	0.9
9 Groundnut (shelled)	4.0	0.4	0.55	0.2
10 Cowpea	2.0	0.4	-	-
11 Green gram	2.0	0.4	-	-
12 Soybean	2.0	0.3	0.75	0.9
13 Pigeonpea	2.0	0.3	-	-
14 Sweet potato	0.2	-	-	-
15 White potato	0.2	-	-	-
16 Cassava	0.2	-	-	-
17 Banana	0.4	-	-	-
18 Sugarcane	0.2	0.1	0.04	0.5
19 Oil palm (kernal)	0.4	-	-	-
20 Cotton (lint)	-		0.25	0.2

The term primary product applies to grain used for the purpose of feeding to animals either directly in an unprocessed form or in a processed form. Main cereals used in Kenya are maize, sorghum, wheat and barley. Direct grain feeding is used mainly at the high level of technology in the dairy and meat production systems with cattle and goat. The intensive livestock industries of poultry and pig production tend to rely on processed feeds.

4.7 Feed Supply Potential (Primary Productivity)

When Part I of the livestock productivity model (Figure 2.1) is applied to the land resources inventory, feed supply potential of each agro-ecological cell are quantified by feed source (Figure 4.1), as described earlier.

Once feed supply potential or primary productivity has been quantified, it is possible to quantify livestock productivity potential of livestock systems at specified performance levels and feed requirements. These aspects are taken into account in Parts II, III, IV and V of the model.

Chapter 5

Characterization of livestock systems

Part II of the livestock productivity model (Figure 2.1) characterizes the livestock systems that are to be considered in assessing secondary productivity potentials. It defines, for three levels of inputs situations (or technology levels), the livestock types, production systems and herd structures.

Of the six types of livestock which are considered in the model, four are considered under pastoral as well as non-pastoral systems. They are: cattle, goat, sheep, camel. The remaining two, poultry and pig, are considered under intensive systems only and without explicitly defining the production systems at this stage in the model development.

Cattle, goat, sheep and camel systems are considered at three inputs levels. The attributes of the three inputs level production circumstances for non-pastoral systems are presented in Table 5.1 and form the basis of the definition of the non-pastoral utilization types considered in the model.

For the pastoral systems, three types of cattle herds have been considered. These are: nomadic distant, nomadic with market access and semi-nomadic, representing respectively the low, intermediate and high level of inputs circumstances. For sheep and goat, two types of herds have been considered. These are: nomadic distant and semi-nomadic, representing respectively the low and high level of inputs circumstances. For camel, one herd type has been considered, representing the normal circumstances of production at a low level of inputs.

Herd structures have been defined in terms of number of heads of animal as well as in terms of reference Tropical Livestock Unit (TLU) defined as a mature animal weighing 250 kg (Houerou and Hoste 1977; Stotz 1983).

Livestock conversion factors for non-pastoral systems in areas with more than 120 days growing period are taken from Stotz (1983). Livestock conversion factors for pastoral systems in areas with less than 120 days growing period are taken from Houerou and Hoste (1977), and are:

Cattle in Herd	= 0.70 TLU	Goat	= 0.08 TLU
Cow	= 1.00 TLU	Donkey	= 0.50 TLU
Sheep	= 0.10 TLU	Camel	= 1.25 TLU

TABLE 5.1
Attributes of the non-pastoral land utilization types considered for livestock production

Attributes	Low inputs	Intermediate inputs	High inputs
Nutrition	Traditional	Mineral supplements, improved calf care, better use of residues and products	As intermediate, plus feeding for optimum economic and biological production; use of primary products
Disease control	None	Current veterinary prophylaxis, plus control or eradication of of diseases or their vectors, e.g., dipping against ticks	As intermediate, plus control of diseases of high performance, e.g., dipping and drenching for mastitis, foot-and-mouth, etc.
Breeding	Selection of unrelated bulls of good conformation, minimum size of heifer at mating	Introduction of adapted exotic breeds and crossbreds	Introduction of graded and exotic breeds of high genetic potential for growth and milk production
Marketing	Low off-take, poor transport facilities, poor processing, including hides and skins	Better off-take, transport and processing, organized markets	Stratified livestock industries, producers receive fair price, organized dairying

5.1 Cattle Systems: Dairy and Meat

At the low level of technology, the systems are characterized by pure Zebu cattle (Stotz 1983). The feed supply is generally native Kikuyu/star grass pastures, and crop residue (maize stover). Cattle are grazed, herded or tethered during the day and kraaled during the night. Cattle are not supplied with concentrates or mineral supplements.

Calves join their dams during milking and for a short while afterwards, during which time they consume the remaining milk in the udder amounting to about 3 to 5 litres per day (400 litres total during the rearing period). Calves are weaned about 5 to 7 months old.

The animals are driven to water at rivers or reservoirs twice a day if nearby, otherwise once a day. Disease control measures are rarely practised, but cattle are compulsorily vaccinated against rinderpest and in some areas against foot and mouth disease.

At the intermediate technology level the cattle would be first generation crossbreds with exotic or high performing grade cattle bred with the help of artificial insemination. Crossbred cattle are generally acquired through upgrading local Zebu cows by Ayrshire, Friesian, Guernsey or Jersey bulls.

Cattle graze natural ley pastures (Kikuyu/star grass) and fields are usually fenced. With regards to feeding, young stock rearing and watering, the same husbandry practice is employed as for Zebu cattle. Crossbred cattle occasionally receive cattle salt, and cattle are regularly dipped or sprayed. Sick animals are treated.

Under the high inputs situations, the systems are based on exotic cattle, Friesian, Ayrshire, Guernsey or Jersey, which have been 'graded' up from the original crosses with indigenous cattle bred back to the exotic type.

Stotz (1983) describes these systems as charaterized by grade cows in a combined grazing/stall feeding system (semi-zero grazing) or complete stall feeding (zero grazing). In the case of the semi zero grazing, cattle usually graze Kikuyu or star grass during the daytime. At night cattle are kraaled or stabled where they are fed with napier and bana grass. Sometimes they are also fed during the day with crop residues and napier grass, particularly during the dry season when pasture productivity is low. Where cattle is permanently housed in a shed, the feed is cut and carried to them. Cattle kept in a zero grazing unit are predominantly fed with napier or bana grass which is first chopped. Dairy cows also receive 20-25 kg/cow per year of mineral supplement, and 500 to 1000 kg/cow per year manufactured and compound concentrates when lactating.

Male and female calves are bucket fed and hand reared. Calves usually receive 270 to 400 litres of milk only until they are weaned within 10 to 18 weeks. When the weaning period is shorter in the case of zero grazing system, calves also receive about 165 kg of concentrates during the rearing period. After this time they depend entirely on forage and join the rest of the herd about 6 months old at a weight of about 160 kg, or at two weeks at a weight of about 35 kg in the zero-grazing system.

Animals are watered twice a day and are regularly dipped or sprayed, drenched against internal parasites and receive other health treatment as needed.

Herd structures parameters are presented for the three cattle herd types in Table 5.2. Base herd structures are defined on the basis of a notional herd of 100 cows.

5.2 Goat Systems: Dairy and Meat

Under the low input technology, the system is characterized by the local small East African goats which are herded or tethered during the day and kept in store, stable or some kind of shelter at night. Goats feed mainly on natural pasture which supply about 70% of all feed consumed. The remainder is obtained for crop residues and through browsing on farm hedges. There is no definite mating season, hence kids are born the whole year round. Kids suckle the mother for about 5 to 7 months and consume the whole amount of milk produced by the dam.

Under the intermediate technology level, the systems are characterized by the dual purpose goats, usually F1 or F2 cross breeds. Generally, an exotic dairy goat buck such as Toggenburg, Saanen or Anglo-Nubian, is used for upgrading local goats. Animals are kept under semi-zero grazing management system. They are tethered during the day, graze mainly natural pasture, and frequently browse shrubs and farm hedges. Goats are penned during the night when they are fed with crop residues and fodder crops like napier grass and maize. Under these feeding conditions, goats obtain approximately 40% of their dry matter requirements from grazing natural pastures. Another 40% is drawn from fodder crops and 20% supplied through feeding crop residues. Animals are sprayed with acaricides regularly and drenched against internal parasites at regular intervals. Lactating females are partially milked before kids are allowed to suckle with an off-take of 1 to 2 kg of milk daily.

TABLE 5.2
Cattle herd structures

| Parameter | Input levels | | | | | |
| | Low | | Intermediate | | High | |
Body weight (kg)	Weight	TLU	Weight	TLU	Weight	TLU
Cows	250	1.00	300	1.25	400	1.75
Replacement heifers (ave. of 1 & 2 yr old)	190	0.76	235	0.94	315	1.26
Calf birth weight	22	0.09	25	0.14	35	0.14
Weaning weight (6 months)	80	0.32	100	0.40	140	0.56
Bulls	300	1.20	-	-	-	-
Number in herds	Head	TLU	Head	TLU	Head	TLU
Cows						
- in milk	67	67	72	95	85	149
- dry	33	33	28	30	15	26
- total	100	100	100	100	100	175
Calves						
- heifers	33	-	36	-	42	-
- bulls	34	-	36	-	(43)	-
- total	67	23.5	72	30.4	(85)42	25.8
Replacement						
- heifers	29	22.0	37	32.0	51	63.8
- bulls	2[1]	1.5	-	-	-	-
- total	31	23.5	37	32.0	51	63.8
Bulls	4	4.8	-	-	-	-
Total	202	151.8	209	187.4	194	264.6

[1] Contribution to meat output accounted for in Table A6.2 under bull calves sold.

TABLE 5.3
Goat herd structures

| Numbers in herd | Input levels | | |
	Low	Intermediate	High
Breeding does	100	100	100
Kids (under 6 months)	127	156	187
Replacement yearlings			
- female	19	25	19
- male	2	2	2
Bucks	4	4	4
Total head	252	287	312
Total adult animals	125	131	125
TLU/adult head	0.10	0.11	0.12
Total TLU	12.5	14.4	15.0

TABLE 5.4
Sheep herd structures

Numbers in herd	Input levels		
	Low	Intermediate	High
Breeding ewes	100	100	100
Lambs (under 6 months)	115	148	178
Replacement yearlings			
- female	19	22	22
- male	2	2	2
Rams	4	3	3
Total head	240	275	305
Total adult animals	125	127	127
TLU/adult head	0.10	0.10	0.10
Total TLU	12.5	12.7	12.7

The high level of technology situation is characterized by the intensive goat production system. The main aim of keeping exotic or grade dairy goats like Toggenburg, Saanen or Anglo-Nubian is to produce milk. Other by-products are sales of breeding stock and goat meat. Goats are usually kept in a zero grazing system, where they are fed with napier grass and other fodder crops along with up to 1.5 kg of concentrate per day. Water is provided in containers which are placed inside the stable.

Kids are bucket fed with milk, obtain 165 litres over a period of 4 months and are supplemented with 50 kg of concentrates. All animals are sprayed with acaricide regularly.

Herd structure parameters are presented for the three goat herd types in Table 5.3. Base herd structures are defined on the basis of a notional herd of 100 does.

5.3   Sheep Systems: Meat and Wool

The dominant local breed kept at the low technology level is the Red Maasai or Red Kikuyu. It is a fat tailed hair sheep weighing some 25 to 30 kg. The animals feed mainly on natural pasture both on the farm and adjacent common land, and use crop residues and other consumable dry matter that can be found. Animals are often tethered during the day and kept in some kind of shelter at night. There is no definite mating season or control over breeding and little health care. Ewes on average lamb once a year. No milk is taken and the only products are meat and wool from surplus male lamb and cull ewes.

At the intermediate level of technology, there is controlled breeding and introduction of better class of sire, usually Droper rams, to improve meat production. The preferred crossbred seems to be 3/4 Droper and 1/4 Maasai. In conjunction with this, there is more frequent joining programme, regular dipping and drenching, improvement in fodder provided and mineral supplementation. These inputs are accompanied by fenced paddocks rather than tethering or sheperding.

At the high level of technology, the production system is characterized by the Red Maasai x Droper crosses for meat and wool production. At higher elevations, (thermal zones T5, T6, T7 and T8), another system dominated by dual purpose wool and meat production, using crossbred wool sheep such as Corriedale-Hampshire, is also considered in the model.

48

A case study of Kenya. Technical Annex 5

TABLE 5.5
Herd proportions by districts of nomadic herds in areas with LGPs <120 days, expressed in TLUs

District	Cattle	Camel	Smallstock	Donkey
Mandera	21.0	65.8	13.0	0.2
Wajir	28.0	64.7	7.0	0.3
Turkana	31.0	29.2	37.5	2.3
Marsabit	54.0	27.5	16.5	2.0
Garissa	76.8	15.6	7.5	0.1
Lamu	76.8	15.6	7.5	0.1
Tana River	66.4	21.0	11.6	1.0
Kiliji	66.4	21.0	11.6	1.0
Isiolo	64.3	16.4	17.5	1.8
Baringo	65.4	12.2	21.9	0.5
Samburu	61.9	6.6	29.3	2.2
Taita Taveta	83.2	-	14.2	2.6
Kwale	83.2	-	14.2	2.6
Kajiado	80.0	-	18.6	1.4
Narok	80.0	-	18.6	1.4

TABLE 5.6
Pastoral cattle herd[1] structures

Numbers in herd	Semi-nomadic	Nomadic with market access	Nomadic distant
Breeding cows			
- in milk	23	23	23
- dry	13	22	22
- total	36	45	45
Replacement heifers (1 to 4 yr. old)	22	22	22
Heifer calves	10	10	10
Sub-total females	68	77	76
Steers 1-2 yrs	7	5	6
2-4 yrs	13	9	4
Bull calves	8	8	5
Bulls	5	5	6
Sub-total males	33	27	21
Herd total	101	104	97
Total TLU	70.7	72.8	67.9

[1] Nomadic distant - low inputs; Nomadic with market access - intermediate inputs; Semi-nomadic - high inputs.

Herd structure parameters are presented for the three sheep herd types in Table 5.4. Base herd structures are defined on the basis of a notional herd of 100 ewes.

5.4 Pastoral Systems: Meat and Milk

Pastoral systems have evolved as a method of producing human food under climatic conditions where normal rainfed crop production is not possible. It operates in the semi-arid zones where the rainfall is low in total quantity and is erratic both geographically over land in time, that is within seasons, and between seasons. The system comprises various combinations of large and small domesticated ruminants with the variations dictated by climate, notably temperature. As a source of food the large ruminants provide milk and some blood and meat while the small ruminants are a source of meat and, in certain locations, of milk. Camels play no part in the market food economy so they are not managed with a view to producing some saleable surplus. The role of the camel is mainly to provide milk and be a beast of burden.

All of the pastoral system operates on various combinations of cattle, camels, sheep and goat with some donkeys as pack animals. The combinations are a function of climate, available herbage and water, and local preferences. In the north the herds are principally camels/smallstock with some cattle in certain locations while in the centre and south the herds are almost exclusively cattle/smallstock. The herd proportions for the principal pastoral districts expressed in TLU equivalent (1 TLU = 250 kg animal) are set out in Table 5.5.

The proposed herd structure for cattle, derived from Unesco (1982), Semenye (1982) and Meadows and White (1981), are presented in Table 5.6. Herd structures for sheep and goat, derived from Unesco (1982), de Leeuw and Peacock (1982), Peacock (1983,1984) and King, Sayers, Peacock and Kontrohr (1982), are presented in Table 5.7. The proposed herd structure for camel is given in Table 5.8.

TABLE 5.7
Pastoral sheep and goat herd[1] structures

Numbers in herd	Semi-nomadic	Nomadic distant
Sheep : Goat ratio	1 : 1.2	1 : 1
Sheep		
- Ewes	50	50
- Ewes weaners	18	13
- Ewes lambs	20	16
Sub-total females	88	79
- Ram lambs	20	15
- Wethers	20	24
- Rams	4	4
Sub-total males	44	43
Total Sheep	132	122
Total TLU	13.2	12.2
Goat		
- Doe	54	60
- Weaner does	18	13
- Kid does	24	18
Sub-total females	96	91
- Kid billies	23	18
- Wethers	33	23
- Billies	4	4
Sub-total males	60	45
Total Goat	156	136
Total TLU	12.5	10.2

[1] Nomadic distant — low inputs; Semi-nomadic — high inputs.

TABLE 5.8
Pastoral camel herd[1] structure

Numbers in herd	Nomadic
Breeding females (6-13 yrs)	
- in milk	21
- dry	21
- total breeders	42
Breeder replacements (2-6 yrs)	22
Female calves	2
Total females	70
Bull calves	4
Bull replacements (2-4 yrs)	13
Bulls (5-12 yrs)	6
Castrates (5-12 yrs)	12
Total males	35
Total Herd	105
Total TLU	131

[1]   Nomadic - low inputs.

Chapter 6

Quantification of herd performance

Part III of the livestock productivity model (Figure 2.1) quantifies livestock productivity potential of each livestock system by quantifying herd performance in acceptable climatic zones.

The thermal zone suitablity ratings for livestock systems are given in Table 6.1. The moisture zone screen, indicating which livestock systems can be considered in which growing period zones, is presented in Table 6.2.

Livestock products per reference herd TLU for cattle, goat, sheep and camel systems at low, intermediate and high levels of technology are presented in Table 6.3 for zones that are considered as S1 for these livestock systems. Where a thermal zone rating is S2, S3 or S4, reference output must be decreased by 25%. 50% and 75% respectively. Where a thermal zone rating is N, the zone is either deemed not suitable because of temperature constraints (and therefore not considered further), or it is deemed not applicable for further consideration because the zone has not been selected for assessment within a particular planning scenario. Where the thermal zone rating is S, as in the case of poultry and pig under intensive system, it represents a screening device to indicate that the zone is deemed suitable for further consideration.

The herd performance calculations for cattle, goat, sheep and camel system are given in the Appendix in Tables A6.1 to A6.24, and these Tables show how output performance values set out in Table 6.3 are derived.

6.1 Cattle Systems: Dairy and Meat

For the cattle systems producing milk and meat, herd performance parameters for the low, intermediate and high technology herds are presented in the Appendix in Table A6.1. The herd performance calculations for the low, intermediate and high technology herds are presented in the Appendix in Tables A6.2, A6.3 and A6.4 respectively. These systems are considered in thermal zones T1, T2, T3, T4, T5, T6, T7 and T8 (Table 6.1) in growing period zones of more than 120 days (Table 6.2).

For the low technology system, output performance per TLU is 264.8 litres milk and 24.6 kg meat. If draught animals were desired then up to 0.09 TLU of draft animals per TLU could be produced but there would be up to 45% proportional reduction in the meat output (Table 6.3).

TABLE 6.1
Suitability ratings for livestock systems by thermal zone

Livestock system	Thermal zone								
	1	2	3	4	5	6	7	8	9
Cattle:									
1 Dairy and meat	S1	S1	S1	S1	S1	S1	S1	S3	N
2 Pastoral	S1	S1	S1	S1	S2	S3	S3	N	N
Goat:									
3 Dairy and meat	S1	S1	S1	S1	S1	S1	S1	S3	N
4 Pastoral	S1	S1	S1	S1	S2	S3	S3	N	N
Sheep:									
5 Meat and wool	S1[1]	S1[1]	S1[1]	S1[1]	S1	S1	S1	S2	N
6 Pastoral	S1	S1	S1	S1	S2	S3	S3	N	N
Camel:									
7 Pastoral	S1	S1	N	N	N	N	N	N	N
Others:									
8 Poultry	S	S	S	S	S	S	S	N	N
9 Pig	S	S	S	S	S	S	S	N	N

[1]   N for wool production in T1,T2,T3,T4 and S2 in T5 and T8 and S1 in T6 nd T7.

TABLE 6.2
Suitability ratings for livestock systems by LGP zone

Livestock system	Length of growing period zone (days)					
	0	1-29	30-59	60-89	90-119	> 120
Cattle:						
1 Dairy and meat	N	N	N	N	N	S
2 Pastoral	S[1]	S[1]	S[1]	S[1,2]	S[1,2]	N
Goat:						
3 Dairy and meat	N	N	N	N	N	S
4 Pastoral	S[1]	S[1]	S[1,2]	S[1,2]	S[1,2]	N
Sheep:						
5 Meat and wool	N	N	N	N	N	S
6 Pastoral	S[1]	S[1]	S[1,2]	S[1,2]	S[1,2]	N
Camel:						
7 Pastoral	S[1]	S[1]	S[1]	S[1]	N	N
Others:						
8 Poultry	N	N	N	N	S	S
9 Pig	N	N	N	N	S	S

[1]   Nomadic   S — Suitable for consideration
[1,2]   Semi-nomadic   N — Not suitable for consideration

For the intermediate technology system, output performance per TLU is 768.4 litres milk and 26.0 kg meat. If draught animals were desired then up to 0.10 TLU of draught animals per TLU could be produced but with up to 49% proportional reduction in meat output (Table 6.3).

For the high technology system, output performance per TLU is 901.5 litres milk and 19.8 kg meat. If draught animals were desired then up to 0.02 TLU of draught animals per TLU could be produced but there would be up to 13% proportional reduction in the meat output (Table 6.3).

TABLE 6.3
Output of livestock products per herd TLU

Livestock system		Input technology		
	Product	Low	Intermediate	High
Cattle:				
1 Dairy and meat	Milk[1]	264.8	567.8	901.5
	Meat[2]	24.6	27.9	19.8
	Draught	0.09	0.1	0.02
2 Pastoral	Milk	59.3	60.0	67.9
	Meat	15.4	18.6	24.6
Goat:				
3 Dairy and meat	Milk	-	263.7	2166.7
	Meat	92.6	114.6	132.7
4 Pastoral	Meat	7.6	13.7	19.8
Sheep:				
5 Meat and wool	Meat	70.5	123.0	145.0
	Wool[3]	11.9	20.8	25.0
6 Pastoral	Meat	8.9	14.2	19.4
Camel:				
7 Pastoral	Milk	96.2	120.6	144.3
	Meat	1.9	2.4	2.9

[1] Milk in litres; Meat in kg dressed weight; Draught animals in TLUs.
[2] Reduce meat output by 45%, 49% and 13% in low, intermediate and high input systems respectively when considering draught animal output.
[3] Wool production in thermal zones T5, T6, T7 and T8 (Table 6.1).

6.2 Goat Systems: Dairy and Meat

For the dairy and meat goat systems, herd performance parameters for the low, intermediate and high technology herds are presented in the Appendix in Table A6.5. The herd performance calculations for the low, intermediate and high technology herds are presented in the Appendix in Tables A6.6, A6.7 and A6.8 respectively. These systems are considered in the thermal zones T1, T2, T3, T4, T5, T6, T7 and T8 (Table 6.1), and in growing period zones of more than 120 days (Table 6.2).

For the low technology system, output performance per TLU is 92.6 kg meat. For the intermediate technology system, output performance per TLU is 263.7 litres milk and 114.6 kg meat. For the high technology system, output performance per TLU is 2166.7 litres of milk and 132.7 kg meat (Table 6.3).

6.3 Sheep Systems: Meat and Wool

For the meat and wool sheep systems, herd performance parameters for the low, intermediate and high technology herds are presented in the Appendix in Table A6.9. The herd performance calculations for the low, intermediate and high technology herds are presented in the Appendix in Tables A6.10, A6.11 and A6.12 respectively. These systems are considered in thermal zones T1, T2, T3, T4, T5, T6, T7 and T8 (Table 6.1), and in growing period zones with more than 120 days (Table 6.2).

For the low technology system, output performance per TLU is 70.5 kg of meat and 11.9 kg wool. For the intermediate technology system, output performance is 123 kg meat and 20.8 kg wool. In the high technology system output performance per TLU is 145.0 kg of meat and 25.0 kg wool (Table 6.3).

6.4 Pastoral Systems: Meat and Milk

6.4.1 *Cattle: meat and milk*

Cattle herd performance parameters for pastoral systems (nomadic distant, nomadic with market access and semi nomadic) are presented in the Appendix in Table A6.13. The herd performance calculations for the low (nomadic distant), intermediate (nomadic with market access) and high (semi-nomadic) technology herds are presented in the Appendix in Tables A6.14, A6.15 and A6.16 respectively.

These systems are considered in thermal zones T1, T2, T3, T4, T5, T6 and T7 (Table 6.1), and in growing period zones less than 119 days (Table 6.2) except for the semi-nomadic herd (high technology) which is considered only in growing period zones 60-89 days and 90-119 days (Table 6.3).

For the nomadic distant herd (low technology), output performance per TLU is 59.3 litres milk and 15.4 kg meat. For the nomadic herd with market access (intermediate technology), output performance per TLU is 60 litres milk and 18.6 kg meat. For the semi-nomadic herd (high technology), output performance per TLU is 67.9 litres milk and 24.6 kg meat (Table 6.3).

6.4.2 *Goat: meat*

Goat herd performance parameters for pastoral systems (nomadic distant and semi-nomadic) are presented in the Appendix in Table A6.17. The herd performance calculations for the nomadic distant and the semi-nomadic herds are presented in the Appendix in Tables A6.18 and A6.19 respectively.

These systems are considered in thermal zones T1, T2, T3, T4, T5, T6 and T7 (Table 6.1). The nomadic distant herd is considered in growing period zones with less than 120 days. The semi-nomadic herd is considered in growing period zones 30-59 days, 60-89 days and 90-120 days (Table 6.2). The nomadic distant and the semi-nomadic herds are presented in the Appendix in Tables A6.18 and A6.19 respectively.

The nomadic distant herd is assumed to represent the low technology system, and its output performance per TLU is 7.6 kg meat. The semi-nomadic herd is assumed to represent the high technology system, and its output performance per TLU is 19.8 kg meat (Table 6.3). The output performance per TLU for the intermediate technology system is assumed to be half-way between the low and the high technology performance (i.e. 13.7 kg meat).

6.4.3 *Sheep: meat*

Sheep herd performance parameters for pastoral systems (nomadic distant and semi-nomadic) are presented in the Appendix in Table A6.20. The herd performance calculations for the nomadic distant and the semi-nomadic herds are presented in the Appendix in Tables A6.21 and A6.22 respectively. These systems are considered in thermal zones T1, T2, T3, T4, T5,

T6 and T7 (Table 6.1). The nomadic distant herd is considered in growing period zones with less than 120 days. The semi-nomadic herd is considered in growing period zones 30-59 days, 60-89 days and 90-119 days (Table 6.2).

The nomadic distant herd is assumed to represent the low technology system, with an output performance per TLU of 8.9 kg meat. The semi-nomadic herd is assumed to represent the high technology system, with an output performance per TLU of 19.4 kg meat (Table 6.3). The output performance at the intermediate level is assumed to be half-way between the low and the high technology performance (i.e. 14.2 kg meat)

6.4.4 *Camel: meat and milk*

Camel herd performance parameters for pastoral system (nomadic) are presented in the Appendix in Table A6.23. The herd performance calculations for this nomadic system are presented in the Appendix in Table A6.24.

The system is considered in thermal zones T1 and T2 (Table 6.1), and in growing period zones less than 90 days (Table 6.2).

The output performance per TLU for the nomadic herd is 96.2 litre milk and 1.9 kg meat (Table 6.3) This output performance per TLU is assumed to apply at the low inputs level. The output performance per TLU at the high inputs level is assumed to be 50% greater (i.e. 144.3 litre milk and 2.9 kg meat), and the intermediate level performance is assumed to be half-way between the low and the high level performance (i.e. 120.6 litre milk and 2.4 kg meat).

6.5 Poultry and Pig: Meat and Egg

Poultry and pig production has been considered to apply only under the intensive system. The feed conversion ratios for poultry meat and eggs and pig meat are given in Section 7. Performance parameters have not been explicitly formulated for poultry and pig system at this stage of the model development but it is envisaged that these would be incorporated at a later stage.

6.6 Pests and Diseases

Major diseases of cattle include rinderpest, trypanosomiasis, contagious bovine pleuropneumonia, dermatophilosis (streoto-thricosis), east coast fever and other tick-borne diseases, and foot and mouth disease. Brucellosis occurs widely and parasitic gastro-enteritis is common, and takes a heavy toll of calves under low management level. Fairly satisfactory control measures for a number of these diseases are available but continued vigilance is necessary to ensure that herds receive protection.

Foot and mouth disease is not important at a low level of production although its occurrence may prevent the export of meat. Ticks can be controlled by dipping or spraying but the provision of facilities and supervision is sometimes difficult.

Sheep and goats are susceptible to a variety of diseases including bacterial pneumonia, internal parasites, foot-rot and in the case of goats caprine pleuropneumonia and in sheep, sheep pox. Treatment is not normally available or sought and losses can be heavy although sick animals are killed and the carcases utilized.

Camels are very susceptible to tick-borne disease and trypanosomiasis. However, they are rarely kept in zones wth more than 90 days growing period.

The distribution of trypanosomiasis and its tse-tse vector in Kenya has been mapped and is included in the land resources data base (Technical Annex 1.1). It has been assumed that in the thermal zones 1, 2, 3 and 4, loss in livestock production performance would be of the order of 75% in the low technology systems and 50% in intermediate and high technology systems due to trypanosomiasis.

Chapter 7

Estimation of feed requirements

Part IV of the livestock productivity model (Figure 2.1) formulates the livestock feed requirements, taking into account maintenance and production needs.

Feed requirements have been formulated to support the herd performances quantified in Section 6 for the individual livestock systems.

In order to support the body's processes and promote production, animals must consume regular supplies of various nutrients. These nutrients may be broadly defined as energy (from carbohydrates and fats), protein, vitamins, minerals and water. They are contained in animal feeds, which are largely of plant origin, in different concentration and combination. Under most intensive systems of animal husbandary, the animal may not always be able to obtain a balanced diet throughout the year because of the seasonal variation in the composition of the herbage.

Water is also needed by the animal, this is obtained from three sources: (a) drunk as water, (b) contained in the herbage or other feed, and (c) resulting from the oxidation of carbohydrates in the tissues. Availability of water is a problem in some parts of Kenya, and much of the pastoral zone has limited permanent water forcing nomadic behaviour. Certain stretches of the country have no water resources. Such a situation must be taken into account in final estimates of livestock carrying capacities. The available sources of information include data which would enable these areas to be identified and measured at the district level and this should be incorporated in the model for a more effective treatment.

A summary of reference feed requirements per herd TLU is given in Table 7.1 for non-pastoral and pastoral systems for three levels of inputs situations. In the non-pastoral systems, intake requirements for cattle, goat and sheep are based on field verification for the herd structures presented in Section 5 for the performance output levels described in Section 6. In the model, crop residue intake in the non-pastoral systems is limited to 30%, 20%, and 10% of total feed intake respectively in the low, intermediate and high technology system.

For pastoral systems, feed requirements are based on Boudet and Riviere (1968) for the herd structures and performances presented in Sections 5 and 6. For poultry and pig, the standard requirements are used (FAO 1988b).

Feed requirements for each system are presented hereunder.

TABLE 7.1
Feed requirements per herd TLU (kg/day dry weight)

Livestock system	Inputs level		
	Low	Intermediate	High
Pastoral (<120 days LGP)			
- Cattle	7.0	7.2	7.4
- Goat	6.6	6.8	7.0
- Sheep	6.6	6.8	7.0
- Camel	6.5	6.6	6.7
Non-pastoral (>120 days LGP)			
- Cattle	7.8	8.5	8.9[1]
- Goat	10.0	11.5	16.1[2]
- Sheep	9.1	11.3	11.6

[1] Includes 1.2 kg/day primary products (3.2 kg/day per lactating cow)
[2] Includes 4.8 kg/day primary products (0.6 kg/day per lactating doe).

7.1 Cattle Systems: Dairy and Meat

In the low technology system, one cow unit requires about 3,740 kg dry matter (DM), corresponding to 1,650 kg total digestable nutrients (TDN) and 210 kg digestible crude protein (DCP) per year, for maintenance and production. These feed requirements are met by grazing Kikuyu/star grass pasture and maize stover.

In the intermediate technology system, one cow unit requires about 5,200 kg DM (2,560 kg TDN and 300 kg DCP per year) for maintenance and production. These feed requirements are met by grazing Kikuyu/star grass pasture and maize stover.

In the high technology system, one cow unit requires about 7,200 kg DM (3500 kg TDN and 420 kg DCP per year) for maintenance and production. This is provided by the napier/bana grass, by feeding maize stover and by feeding 1,165 kg concentrates.

The above requirements correspond to 7.8, 8.5 and 8.9 kg/day per reference herd TLU for the low, intermediate and high technology systems respectively (Table 7.1)

7.2 Goat Systems: Dairy and Meat

In the low technology system, one doe unit requires about 470 kg DM per year, provided by natural pasture.

In the intermediate technology system, one doe unit requires about 700 kg DM per year. This is provided by a combination of sources: natural pasture (280 kg), fodder crops (280 kg) and crop residue (140 kg).

In the high technology system, one doe unit requires about 960 kg DM per year. This is provided by fodder crops (610 kg), crop residue (140 kg) and concentrates (210 kg).

The above requirements correspond to 10.0, 11.5 and 16.1 kg/year per reference herd TLU for the low, intermediate and high technology systems respectively (Table 7.1).

7.3 Sheep Systems: Meat and Wool

In the low technology system, one ewe unit requires about 360 kg DM per year, provided by natural pasture.

In the intermediate technology system, one ewe unit requires about 610 kg DM per year. This is provided by a combination of sources: natural pasture, fodder crops and crop residue.

In the high technology system, one ewe unit requires about 750 kg DM per year. This is provided by natural pasture, fodder crops, crop residue and concentrates.

The above requirements correspond to 9.1, 11.3 and 11.6 kg/year per reference herd TLU for the low, intermediate and high technology systems respectively (Table 7.1).

7.4 Pastoral Systems: Milk and Meat

For the pastoral systems (< 120 days growing period), feed requirements are based on a daily intake of 2.5 kg dry matter per 100 kg liveweight or 6.25 kg dry matter for the 250 kg reference TLU. Maintenance requirements are 2.9 FU/day and 160 g/day digestible protein (DP). The annual maintenance dietary needs of a reference TLU are thus 1,060 FU or 2,280 kg DM (1FU = 2.15 kg DM) and 58 kg DP. Production requirements are in addition at 350 extra FU/year (0.95 FU/day) and 28 kg DP (75 g/day) for weight gain of 100 kg/year (300 g/day) or a production of 1,000 kg/year(2.74 kg/day) of milk.

The above requirements correspond to 7.0, 7.2 and 7.4 kg DM/day per TLU for the low, intermediate and high technology systems respectively for cattle; 6.6, 6.8 and 7.0 kg DM/day per TLU for goat and sheep; and 6.5, 6.6 and 6.7 kg DM/day per TLU for camel (Table 7.1).

7.5 Poultry and Pig: Meat and Egg

These animals are considered only under the intensive systems and standard requirements are used (FAO 1988b). For poultry these are 2.5 kg of feed (primary products) for 1 kg of meat, and 3,5 kg of feed for 1 kg of egg mass. For pig it is 4 kg of feed for 1 kg of meat.

Chapter 8

Livestock productivity potential

Part V of the livestock productivity model (Figure 2.1) deals with quantification of livestock productivity potential (secondary productivity) of land (agro-ecological cells). This is achieved by setting feed requirements of livestock systems from Part IV against feed supply from Part I.

However, before it is possible to set feed requirements against feed supply, the latter from its various sources as applicable must be quantified by agro-ecological cell in relation to the objective function driving the model.

The permissible thermal and LGP zones for the different livestock systems is taken from the Tables 6.1 and 6.2, and the expected output of the products per herd TLU is taken from Table 6.3 for cattle, goat, sheep and camel, and from Section 7.5 for poultry and pig. Where output performance is assumed to be affected by constraints such as temperature stress, tse-tse, the expected loss in performance output is taken into account.

References

Blair Rains A. and Kassam A.H. 1980. Land resources and animal production. Working Paper No. 8. Report on the Second FAO/UNFPA Expert Consultation on 'Land Resources for Populations of the Future'. FAO, Rome.

Boonman J.G. 1979. Developments of cultivated pastures in the highlands of East Africa. Ministry of Agriculture, Republic of Kenya, Nairobi.

Boudet G. and Riviere R. 1968. Emploi practique des analyses fourrageres pour l'appreciation des pasturages tropicaux. Revue d'Elevage et de Medecine Veterinaire des Pays Tropicaux, 211: 227-266.

Edwards D.C. and Bogdan A.V. 1968. Importance of grassland plants of Kenya. Sir Isaac Pitman and Sons Ltd., Nairobi.

FAO. 1976. Framework for Land Evaluation. Soils Bulletin 32. FAO, Rome.

FAO. 1978. Report on the Agro-ecological Zones Project. Vol. 1. Methodology and results for Africa. World Soil Resources Report 48/1, FAO, Rome.

FAO. 1980. Land Resources for Populations of the Future. Report of the Second FAO/UNFPA Expert Consultation. FAO, Rome.

FAO. 1984. Population supporting capacity assesment of Kenya. Mission Report.AGL-FAO, Rome.

FAO. 1988a. FAO Guidelines: Land Evaluation for Extensive Grazing. FAO Soils Bulletin 58. FAO, Rome.

FAO. 1988b. A seminar on Pig Production in the Tropics and Sub-tropical Regions, (Nils R. Standal, ed.). Suchow, China 21-25 September 1987. FAO, Rome.

Fischer G.W., Shah M.M., Kassam A.H. and van Velthuizen H.T. 1989. Systems Documentation Guide to Computer Programs for Land Productivity Assessments. Technical Annex 7. Agroecological Land Resources Assessment for Agricultural Development Planning, a Case Study of Kenya. AGL-FAO/ IIASA, Rome.

Fischer G.W., Shah M.M., Kassam A.H. and van Velthuizen H.T. 1989. Crop Productivity Assessment: Results at District Level. Technical Annex 8. Agroecological Land Resources Assessment for Agricultural Development Planning, a Case Study of Kenya. AGL-FAO/IIASA, Rome.

Hammer W.I. 1981. Soil Conservation Consultant Report. Technical Note No.7, Centre for Soil Research, Bogor, Indonesia.

Houerou H.N. Le and Hoste C.H. 1977. Rangeland production and annual rainfall relations in the Mediterranean Basin and the African Sahelo-Sudanian Zone. J. Range Magt. 30: 181-189.

Jaetzold R. and Schmidt H. 1982. Farm Management Handbook of Kenya. Volume II. Parts A, B and C. Ministry of Agriculture in Cooperation with German Agency for Technical Cooperation, Nairobi.

Kassam A.H. 1977. Net biomass and yields of crops. Consultant's Report. Agro-ecological Zones Project. AGL-FAO, Rome.

Kassam A.H. Kowal J.M. and Sarraf S. 1977. Climatic adaptability of crops. Consultants' Report. Agro-ecological Zones Project. AGL/FAO, Rome.

Kassam A.H., van Velthuizen H.T., Fischer G.W. and Shah M.M. 1989. Land Resources. Technical Annex 1. Agroecological Land Resources Assessment for Agricultural Development Planning, a Case Study of Kenya. AGL-FAO/IIASA, Rome.

Kassam A.H., van Velthuizen H.T., Mitchell A.J.B., Fischer G.W. and Shah M.M. 1989. Soil Erosion and Productivity. Technical Annex 2. Agroecological Land Resources Assessment for Agricultural Development Planning, a Case Study of Kenya. AGL-FAO/IIASA, Rome.

Kassam A.H., van Velthuizen H.T., Fischer G.W. and Shah M.M. 1989. Agro-climatic and Agro-edaphic Suitabilities for Barley, Oat, Cowpea, Green gram and Pigeonpea. Technical Annex 3. Agroecological Land Resources Assessment for Aricultural Development Planning, a Case Sudy of Kenya. AGL-FAO/IIASA, Rome.

Kassam A.H., van Velthuizen H.T., Fischer G.W. and Shah M.M. 1989. Crop Productivity. Technical Annex 4. Agroecological Land Resources Assessment for Agricultural Development Planning, a Case Study of Kenya. AGL-FAO/IIASA, Rome.

Kassam A.H., van Velthuizen H.T., Singh K.D., Fischer G.W. and Shah M.M. 1989. Fuelwood Productivity. Technical Annex 6. Agroecological Land Resources Assessment for Agricultural Development Planning, a Case Study of Kenya. AGL-FAO/IIASA, Rome.

King J.M. Sayers A.F. Peacock C.P. and Kontrohr E. 1982. Maasai herd and flock structure in relation to household livestock wealth and group ranch development. Working Document No. 27. ILCA, Kenya.

Leeuw P.N. de and Peacock C.P. 1982. The productivity of small ruminants in the Maasai Pastoral System in Kajiado District of Kenya. Working Document No. 25. ILCA, Kenya.

Meadows S.J. and White J.M. 1981. Cattle structure in Kenya's pastoral rangelands. Pastoral Network Paper 11e. Overseas Development Institute, London.

Mitchell A.J.B. 1986. Soil Erosion and Conservation. Consultant's Report. AGL-FAO, Rome.

Peacock C.P. 1983. A rapid appraisal of goat and sheep flock demography in East and West Africa. Method, results and application to livestock research and development. Working Document No 28. ILCA, Kenya.

Peacock C.P. 1984. Sheep and goat production on Maasai group ranches Ph.D. Thesis. University of Reading, UK.

Rattray J.M. 1960. The grass cover of Africa. FAO, Rome.

Semenye P.P. 1980. A preliminary report of cattle productivity in Olkarkar, Merueshi and Mbirikani group ranches. ILCA, Kenya.

Stotz D. 1983. Production Techniques and Economics of Smallholder Livestock Production Systems in Kenya. Farm Management Handbook of Kenya IV. Ministry of Agriculture Republic of Kenya, Nairobi.

Unesco. 1982. Resource management for the Rendille Area of Northern Kenya. Integrated Project on Arid Lands (IPAL), Marsabit.

Wischmeier W.H. and Smith D.D. 1978. Predicting rainfall erosion losses. United States Department of Agriculture Handbook No. 536.

Wit C.T. de. 1965. Photosynthesis of leaf canopies. Agricultural Research Report 663. Centre for Agricultural Publications and Documentation, Wageningen.

Appendix

Herd performance parameters and calculations

TABLE A6.1
Herd performance parameters for the dairy and meat cattle systems

Parameters	Inputs level		
	Low	Intermediate	High
Fertility rate	0.67	0.72	0.85
Prolificacy rate	1	1	1
Bulls per cow	0.03	0	0
Milk yield per lactation in tonnes	0.6	2.0	2.8
Fraction of females milked	1	1	1
Cow mortality rate[1]	0.03	0.06	0.06
Bull mortality rate	0.05	0	0
Female replacement mortality rate[1]	0.05	0.07	0.09
Male replacement mortality rate	0.05	0	0
Female young mortality rate	0.25	0.20	0.10
Male young mortality rate	0.25	0.20	0.10
Other stock mortality rate	0.07	0.05	0.06
Female breeder carcase weight (tonnes)	0.125	0.156	0.208
Male breeded carcase weight (tonnes)	0.150	0	0
Carcase weight of other stock (tonnes)	0.080	0.094	0.104
Presence of males in the system	yes	no	no

[1]   Increase in mortality rate with increase in inputs due to relatively greater susceptibility of crossbred and grade cattle to local pests and diseases.

TABLE A6.2
Herd performance calculations for the dairy and meat cattle system at low inputs

Base herd structure		Transfers	Output	
Breeding cows		Death rate 3%		
3 year old	14	+ 14 recruits from		
4 year old	13	replacement herd		
5 year old	13			
6 year old	13	- 3 deaths		
7 year old	12			
8 year old	12	- 11 culls x 250 kg LW	2750	kg LW
9 year old	12			
10 year old	<u>11</u>			
	100			
Calves under 1 year		67% calving rate		
Heifers	33	Death rate 25%		
		- 8 deaths		
		- 15 recruits to heifer		
		replacement herd		
		- 10 sales @ 135 kg	1350	kg LW
Bulls	<u>34</u>	Death rate 25%		
		- 9 deaths		
		- 25 sales @ 135 kg	<u>3375</u>	kg LW
	67			
Replacement heifers		Death rate 5%		
1 year old	15	+ 15 recruits from calf herd		
2 year old	<u>14</u>	- 1 death		
	29	- 14 recruits to cow herd		
Total meat output			7475	kg LW
			or 3737.5	kg DW
Total milk output (67 cows x 600 litres)			40 200 litres	
Production		Milk	Meat	
per cow		402 litres	37.37 kg DW	
per TLU		264.8 litres	24.6 kg DW	

Total TLU = 151.8 (Table 5.2)

TABLE A6.3
Herd performance calculations for the dairy and meat cattle system at intermediate inputs

Base herd structure		Transfers	Output	
Breeding cows		Death rate 6%		
3 year old	17	+ 17 recruits from		
4 year old	16	replacement herd		
5 year old	16			
6 year old	15	- 6 deaths		
7 year old	13			
8 year old	12	- 11 culls x 300 kg LW	3300	kg LW
9 year old	11			
	100			
Calves under 1 year		72% calving rate		
Heifers	36	Death rate 20%		
		- 7 deaths		
		- 20 recruits to heifer		
		replacement herd		
		- 9 sales @ 170 kg	1530	kg LW
Bulls	36	Death rate 20%		
		- 7 deaths		
		- 29 sales @ 170 kg	4930	kg LW
	72			
Replacement heifers		Death rate 7%		
1 year old	20	+ 20 recruits from calf herd		
2 year old	17	- 3 deaths		
	37	- 17 recruits to cow herd		
Total meat output			9760 or 3737.5	kg LW kg DW
Total milk output (72 cows x 2000 litres)			144 000 litres	
Production		Milk	Meat	
per cow		1440 litres	48.8 kg DW	
per TLU		768.4 litres	26.0 kg DW	

Total TLU = 187.4 (Table 5.2)

TABLE A6.4
Herd performance calculations for the dairy and meat cattle system at high inputs

Base herd structure	Transfers	Output	
Breeding cows	Death rate 6%		
3 year old 23	+ 23 recruits from		
4 year old 21	replacement herd		
5 year old 20			
6 year old 19	- 6 deaths		
7 year old <u>17</u>			
100	- 17 culls x 400 kg LW	6800	kg LW
Calves under 1 year	85% calving rate		
Heifers 42	Death rate 10%		
	- 4 deaths		
	- 28 recruits to heifer		
	replacement herd		
	- 10 sales @ 230 kg	2300	kg LW
Bulls <u>43</u>	Death rate 10%		
	- 4 deaths		
	- 39 sales @ 35 kg	<u>1365</u>	kg LW
85	(2 weeks old)		
Replacement heifers	Death rate 10%		
1 year old 28	+ 28 recruits from calf herd		
2 year old <u>23</u>	- 5 deaths		
51	- 23 recruits to cow herd		
Total meat output		10465	kg LW
		or 5232.5	kg DW
Total milk output (85 cows x 2800 litres)		238 000 litres	
Production	Milk	Meat	
per cow	2380 litres	52.3 kg DW	
per TLU	901.5 litres	19.8 kg DW	

Total TLU = 264.6 (Table 5.2)

TABLE A6.5

Herd performance parameters for the dairy and meat goat systems

Parameters	Inputs level		
	Low	Intermediate	High
Fertility rate	1.27	1.56	1.875
Prolificacy rate	1.02	1.25	1.50
Bucks per doe	0.04	0.033	0.025
Milk yield per lactation in tonnes	0	0.03	0.26
Fraction of females milked	0	0.95	1
Doe mortality rate	0.06	0.06	0.06
Buck mortality rate	0.06	0.06	0.06
Female replacement mortality rate	0.1	0.1	0.1
Male replacement mortality rate	0.1	0.1	0.1
Female young mortality rate	0.15	0.12	0.10
Male young mortality rate	0.15	0.12	0.10
Other stock mortality rate	0.1	0.1	0.1
Female breeder carcase weight (tonnes)	0.014	0.017	0.020
Male breeded carcase weight (tonnes)	0.02	0.022	0.023
Carcase weight of other stock (tonnes)	0.012	0.015	0.018
Presence of males in the system	yes	yes	yes

TABLE A6.6
Herd performance calculations for the dairy and meat goat system at low inputs

Base herd structure		Transfers	Output	
Breeding does		Death rate 6%		
2 year old	17	+ 17 recruits from		
3 year old	16	replacement flock		
4 year old	16			
5 year old	15	- 6 deaths		
6 year old	13			
7 year old	12	- 11 culls x 28 kg LW	308	kg LW
8 year old	11			
	100			
Kidding effective rate 127%/doe/year				
Female	63	Death rate 15%		
		- 9 deaths		
		- 19 recruits to replacement flock		
		- 35 surplus for sale as yearlings @ 20 kg LW	700	kg LW
Male	64	Death rate 15%		
		- 10 deaths		
		- 2 recruits to replacement flock		
		- 52 surplus for sale as yearlings @ 24 kg LW	1248	kg LW
	127			
Replacement yearlings		Death rate 10%		
Does 1 year old	19	+ 19 recruits		
		- 2 deaths		
		- 17 recruits to breeding flock		
Bucks 1 year old	2	+ 2 recruits		
		- 1 to breeding herd		
	21	- 1 cull sold @ 40 kg LW	40	kg LW
Bucks		Death rate 6%		
2 year old	1	+ 1 recruit		
3 year old	1	- 0.5 i.e. 1 death every second year		
4 year old	1			
5 year old	1	- 0.5 cull sold @ 40 kg LW	20	kg LW
	4			
Total meat output			2316	kg LW
			or 1158	kg DW
Production		Meat		
per doe		11.58 kg DW		
per TLU		92.64 kg DW		

Total TLU = 12.5 (Table 5.3)

TABLE A6.7
Herd performance calculations for the dairy and meat goat system at intermediate inputs

Base herd structure		Transfers	Output	
Breeding does		Death rate 6%		
2 year old	23	+ 23 recruits from		
3 year old	21	replacement flock		
4 year old	20			
5 year old	19	- 6 deaths		
6 year old	17			
	100	- 17 culls x 34 kg LW	578	kg LW
Kidding effective rate 156%/doe/year				
Female	78	Death rate 12%		
		- 9 deaths		
		- 23 recruits to replacement flock		
		- 46 sales @ 22 kg LW	1012	kg LW
Male	78	Death rate 12%		
		- 10 deaths		
		- 2 recruits to buck replacement flock		
		- 66 sales @ 25 kg LW	1650	kg LW
	156			
Replacement yearlings		Death rate 10%		
Does 1 year old	25	- 2 deaths		
		- 23 recruits to breeding flock		
Bucks 1 year old	2	+ 2 from kids flock		
		- 1 to breeding herd		
		- 1 cull sold @ 40 kg LW	40	kg LW
	27			
Bucks		Death rate 6%		
2 year old	1	+ 1 recruit		
3 year old	1	- 0.5 i.e. 1 death every second year		
4 year old	1			
5 year old	1	- 0.5 cull sold @ 44 kg LW	22	kg LW
	4			
Total meat output			3302	kg LW
			or 1651	kg DW
Milk production 180 litres/lactation;				
Less: allowance for kids 150 litres/lactation;				
Net milk output:				
30 litres x 1.25 lactation = 38 litres/doe/year lactation				
Total milk output for 100 doe herd:			3800 litres	
Production		Milk	Meat	
per doe		38 litres	16.51 kg DW	
per TLU		263.7 litres	114.60 kg DW	

Total TLU = 14.4 (Table 5.3)

TABLE A6.8
Herd performance calculations for the dairy and meat goat system at high inputs

Base herd structure		Transfers	Output	
Breeding does		Death rate 6%		
2 year old	17	+ 17 recruits from		
3 year old	16	replacement flock		
4 year old	15			
5 year old	14	- 6 deaths		
6 year old	14			
7 year old	13	- 11 culls x 40 kg LW	440	kg LW
8 year old	<u>11</u>			
	100			
Kidding effective rate 187.5%/doe/year				
Female	93	Death rate 10%		
		- 9 deaths		
		- 19 recruits to replacement flock		
		- 65 sales @ 22 kg LW	1430	kg LW
Male	<u>94</u>	Death rate 10%		
		- 10 deaths		
		- 2 recruits to buck replacement flock		
		- 82 sales @ 25 kg LW	2050	kg LW
	187			
Replacement yearlings		Death rate 10%		
Does 1 year old	19	+ 19 recruits		
		- 2 deaths		
		- 17 recruits to breeding flock		
Bucks 1 year old	<u>2</u>	+ 2 recruits		
		- 1 to breeding herd		
		- 1 cull sold @ 40 kg LW	40	kg LW
	21			
Bucks		Death rate 6%		
2 year old	1	+ 1 recruit		
3 year old	1	- 0.5 i.e. 1 death every		
4 year old	1	second year		
5 year old	<u>1</u>	- 0.5 cull sold @ 44 kg LW	<u>22</u>	kg LW
	4			
Total meat output			3982	kg LW
			or 1991	kg DW
Milk production 425 litres/lactation;				
Less: allowance for kids 165 litres/lactation;				
Net milk output:				
260 litres x 1.25 lactation = 325 litres/doe/year lactation				
Total milk output for 100 doe herd:			32 500 litres	
Production		Milk	Meat	
per doe		325 litres	19.91 kg DW	
per TLU		2166.7 litres	132.73 kg DW	

Total TLU = 15 (Table 5.3)

TABLE A6.9
Herd performance parameters for the meat and wool sheep systems

Parameters	Inputs level		
	Low	Intermediate	High
Fertility rate	1.00	1.25	1.25
Prolificacy rate	1.15	1.18	1.20
Rams per ewe	0.04	0.033	0.033
Milk yield per lactation in tonnes	0	0	0
Fraction of females milked	0	0	0
Ewe mortality rate[1]	0.06	0.07	0.07
Ram mortality rate[1]	0.06	0.07	0.07
Female replacement mortality rate	0.1	0.1	0.1
Male replacement mortality rate	0.1	0.1	0.1
Female young mortality rate	0.17	0.1	0.1
Male young mortality rate	0.17	0.1	0.1
Other stock mortality rate	0	0	0
Female breeder carcase weight (tonnes)	0.014	0.018	0.020
Male breeded carcase weight (tonnes)	0.018	0.022	0.022
Carcase weight of other stock (tonnes)	0.010	0.013	0.015
Presence of males in the system	yes	yes	yes

[1] Increase in mortality rate with increase in inputs due to relatively greater susceptibility of crossbred and grade animals to local pests and diseases.

TABLE A6.10
Herd performance calculations for the meat and wool sheep system at low inputs

Base herd structure		Transfers	Output	
Breeding ewes		Death rate 6%		
2 year old	17	+ 17 recruits from		
3 year old	16	replacement flock		
4 year old	16			
5 year old	15	- 6 deaths		
6 year old	13			
7 year old	12	- 11 culls x 28 kg LW	308	kg LW
8 year old	11			
	100			
Lambing effective rate 115%/ewe/year				
Female	58	Death rate 17%		
		- 10 deaths		
		- 19 recruits to replacement flock		
		- 29 sales @ 18 kg LW		
			522	kg LW
Male	57	Death rate 17%		
		- 10 deaths		
		- 2 recruits to replacement flock		
		- 45 sales @ 20 kg LW	900	kg LW
	115			
Replacement yearlings		Death rate 10%		
Ewes 1 year old	19	+ 19 recruits		
		- 2 deaths		
		- 17 recruits to breeding flock		
Rams 1 year old	2	- 1 to breeding herd		
		- 1 cull sold @ 30 kg LW		
	21	every second year	15	kg LW
Rams		Death rate 6%		
2 year old	1	+ 1 recruit		
3 year old	1	- 0.5 i.e. 1 death every		
4 year old	1	second year		
5 year old	1	- 0.5 cull sold @ 36 kg LW	18	kg LW
	4			
Total meat output			1763	kg LW
			or 882	kg DW
Total wool output (1.2 kg per adult head)			149 kg	

Production	Meat	Wool
per ewe	8.82 kg DW	1.49 kg
per TLU	70.5 kg DW	11.9 kg

Total TLU = 12.5 (Table 5.4)

TABLE A6.11
Herd performance calculations for the meat and wool sheep system at intermediate inputs

Base herd structure		Transfers	Output	
Breeding ewes		Death rate 7%		
2 year old	20	+ 20 recruits from		
3 year old	19	replacement flock		
4 year old	17			
5 year old	16	- 7 deaths		
6 year old	15			
7 year old	<u>13</u>	- 13 culls x 36 kg LW	468	kg LW
	100			
Lambing effective rate 148%/ewe/year				
Female	74	Death rate 10%		
		- 8 deaths		
		- 22 recruits to replacement flock		
		- 44 sales @ 22 kg LW	968	kg LW
Male	<u>74</u>	Death rate 10%		
		- 7 deaths		
		- 2 recruits to replacement flock		
		- 65 sales @ 25 kg LW	1625	kg LW
	148			
Replacement yearlings		Death rate 10%		
Ewes 1 year old	22	+ 22 recruits		
		- 2 deaths		
		- 20 recruits to breeding flock		
Rams 1 year old	<u>2</u>	+ 2 recruits		
		- 1 to breeding herd		
		- 1 cull @ 40 kg LW	40	kg LW
	24			
Rams		Death rate 10%		
2 year old	1	+ 1 recruit		
3 year old	1	- 0.5 death/ year		
4 year old	<u>1</u>	- 0.5 cull sold @ 46 kg LW	<u>23</u>	kg LW
	3			
Total meat output			3124	kg LW
			or 1562	kg DW
Total wool output (2.0 kg per adult head)			264 kg	
Production		Meat	Wool	
per ewe		15.62 kg DW	2.64 kg	
per TLU		123.0 kg DW	20.8 kg	

Total TLU = 12.7 (Table 5.4)

TABLE A6.12
Herd performance calculations for the meat and wool sheep system at high inputs

Base herd structure		Transfers	Output	
Breeding ewes		Death rate 7%		
2 year old	20	+ 20 recruits from		
3 year old	19	replacement flock		
4 year old	17			
5 year old	16	- 7 deaths		
6 year old	15			
7 year old	13	- 13 culls x 40 kg LW	520	kg LW
	100			
Lambing effective rate 178%/ewe/year				
Female	89	Death rate 10%		
		- 8 deaths		
		- 22 recruits to replacement flock		
		- 58 sales @ 22 kg LW	1276	kg LW
Male	89	Death rate 10%		
		- 9 deaths		
		- 2 recruits to replacement flock		
		- 73 sales @ 25 kg LW	1825	kg LW
	178			
Replacement yearlings		Death rate 10%		
Ewes 1 year old	22	+ 22 recruits		
		- 2 deaths		
		- 20 recruits to breeding flock		
Rams 1 year old	2	+ 1 recruits		
		- 1 to breeding herd		
		- 1 cull @ 40 kg LW	40	kg LW
	24			
Rams		Death rate 10%		
2 year old	1	+ 1 recruit		
3 year old	1	- 0.5 death/year		
4 year old	1	- 0.5 cull sold @ 46 kg LW	23	kg LW
	3			
Total meat output			3684	kg LW
			or 1842	kg DW
Total wool output (2.5 kg per adult head)			317.5 kg	
Production		Meat	Wool	
per ewe		18.42 kg DW	3.17 kg	
per TLU		145.0 kg DW	25 kg	

Total TLU = 12.7 (Table 5.4)

TABLE A6.13
Herd performance parameters for the cattle pastoral systems

Parameters	Semi-nomadic	Nomadic with market access	Nomadic distant
Fertility rate	0.67	0.50	0.50
Prolificacy rate	1	1	1
Bulls per cow	0.1	0.1	0.18
Milk yield per lactation in tonnes	0.2	0.18	0.18
Fraction of females milked	0.65	0.45	0.4
Cow mortality rate	0.05	0.06	0.09
Bull mortality rate	0.05	0.07	0.10
Female replacement mortality rate	0.05	0.05	0.05
Male replacement mortality rate	0.05	0.07	0.10
Female young mortality rate	0.12	0.17	0.17
Male young mortality rate	0.12	0.17	0.17
Female breeder carcase weight (tonnes)	0.125	0.125	0.125
Male breeded carcase weight (tonnes)	0.16	0.14	0.13
Carcase weight of other stock (tonnes)	0.1	0.15	0.20
Presence of males in the system	yes	yes	yes

TABLE A6.14

Herd performance calculations for the cattle pastoral system (nomadic distant) at low inputs

Base herd structure		Transfers	Output	
Breeding cows		Death rate 3%		
4 year old	8	+ 7 recruits herd		
5 year old	8			
6 year old	7			
7 year old	7	- 4 deaths		
8 year old	6			
9 year old	5			
10 year old	4	- 31 culls x 250 kg LW	750	kg LW
	45			
Calves under 1 year		50% calving rate		
Heifer (born)	11	Death rate 17%		
Net live calves	9	- 2 deaths		
		- 8 heifer herd		
		- 1 slaughtered @ 50 kg LW	50	kg LW
Replacement heifers		Death rate 5%		
1 year old	8	+ 8 recruits		
2 year old	7	- 1 death		
3 year old	7	- 7 recruits to cow herd		
	22			
Bull calves		Death rate 17%		
Bull calves (born).	12	- 2 deaths		
Net live calves	10	- 2 to bull herd		
		- 3 to steer herd		
		- 5 slaughtered @ 50 k LW	250	kg LW
Steer herd		Death rate 10%		
1 year old	3	+ 3 recruits		
2 year old	3	- 1 death		
3 year old	2	- 2 slaughtered @ 300 kg LW	600	kg LW
4 year old	2			
	10			
Bulls				
1 year old	2	+ 2 recruits		
2 year old	2	- 1 death		
3 year old	-			
4 year old	1			
5 year old	-			
6 year old	1	- 1 cull @ 300 kg LW	300	kg LW
	6			
Total meat output			1950	kg LW
			or 1044	kg DW
Total milk output (45 cows at 50% calving = 23 x 175 litres)			4025 litres	

Production	Milk	Meat
per TLU	59.3 litres	15.4 kg DW

Total TLU = 67.9 (Table 5.6

TABLE A6.15
Herd performance calculations for the cattle pastoral system (nomadic distant) at intermediate inputs

Base herd structure		Transfers	Output	
Breeding cows		Death rate 6%		
4 year old	8	+ 7 recruits herd		
5 year old	8			
6 year old	7	- 3 deaths		
7 year old	7			
8 year old	6			
9 year old	5			
10 year old	4	- 4 culls x 250 kg LW	1000	kg LW
	45			
Calves under 1 year		50% calving rate		
Heifer	12	Death rate 17%		
Net live	10	- 2 deaths		
calves		- 8 heifer herd		
		- 2 slaughtered @ 50 kg LW	100	kg LW
Replacement heifers		Death rate 5%		
1 year old	8	+ 8 recruits		
2 year old	7	- 1 death		
3 year old	7	- 7 recruits to cow herd		
	22			
Bull calves		Death rate 17%		
Bull calves	11	- 2 deaths		
Net live	9	- 1 to bull herd		
calves		- 5 to steer herd		
		- 3 slaughtered @ 50 k LW	150	kg LW
Steer herd		Death rate 7%		
1 year old	5	+ 5 recruits		
2 year old	5	- 1 death		
3 year old	4	- 4 slaughtered @ 300 kg LW	1200	kg LW
	14			
Bulls				
1 year old	1	+ 1 recruits		
2 year old	1			
3 year old	1	- 1 death or 1 slaughtered in		
4 year old	1	alternate years		
5 year old	1	0.5 @ 300 kg	150	kg LW
	5			
Total meat output			2600	kg LW
			or 1353	kg DW
Total milk output (45 cows at 50% calving = 23 x 190 litres)			4370 litres	
Production		Milk	Meat	
per TLU		60.0 litres	18.6 kg DW	

Total TLU = 72.8 (Table 5.6)

TABLE A6.16
Herd performance calculations for the cattle pastoral system (nomadic distant) at high inputs

Base herd structure		Transfers	Output	
Breeding cows		Death rate 5%		
4 year old	7	+ 7 recruits		
5 year old	7			
6 year old	6			
7 year old	6	- 2 deaths		
8 year old	5			
9 year old	5	- 5 culls x 250 kg LW	1250	kg LW
	36			
Calves under 1 year		67% calving rate		
Heifer	12	Death rate 12%		
Net live	10	- 2 deaths		
calves		- 8 to heifer herd		
		- 2 slaughtered @ 50 kg LW	100	kg LW
Replacement heifers		Death rate 5%		
1 year old	8	+ 8 recruits		
2 year old	7	- 1 death		
3 year old	7	- 7 recruits to cow herd		
	22			
Bull calves		Death rate 12%		
Bull calves	12	- 1 death		
Net live rate	9	- 1 to bull herd		
		- 7 to steer herd		
		- 3 slaughtered @ 50 k LW	150	kg LW
Steer herd		Death rate 5%		
1 year old	7	- 1 to bull herd		
2 year old	7	- 7 to steer herd		
3 year old	6	+ 7 recruits		
	20	- 1 death		
		- 6 slaughtered @ 300 kg LW	1800	kg LW
Bulls				
1 year old	1	+ 1 recruits		
2 year old	1			
3 year old	1	- 1 death or 1 slaughtered in		
4 year old	1	alternate years		
5 year old	1	0.5 @ 350 kg	175	kg LW
	5			
Total meat output			3475	kg LW
			or 1737.5	kg DW
Total milk output (45 cows at 67% calving = 24 x 200 litres)			4800 litres	
Production		Milk	Meat	
per TLU		67.9 litres	24.6 kg DW	

Total TLU = 70.6 (Table 5.6)

TABLE A6.17

Herd performance parameters for the goat pastoral systems

Parameters	Semi-nomadic	Nomadic distant
Female breeder mortality rate	0.15	0.25
Male breeder mortality rate	0.25	0.25
Female replacement mortality rate	0.3	0.3
Male replacement mortality rate	0.3	0.3
Young mortality rate	0.25	0.3
Fertility rate	0.6	0.4
Prolificacy rate	1.45	1.45
Breeder females per male	13.5	15
Female breeder carcase weight (tonnes)	0.028	0.025
Male breeder carcase weight (tonnes)	0.045	0.04
Slaughter stock carcase weight (tonnes)	0.04	0.03
Milk yield per lactation (tonnes)	0	0
Fraction of females milked	0	0

TABLE A6.18
Herd performance calculations for the goat pastoral system (nomadic distant) at low inputs

Base herd structure		Transfers	Output	
Does		Death rate 25%		
2 year old	12	+ 15 recruits		
3 year old	12	- 15 deaths		
4 year old	11			
5 year old	11			
6 year old	8			
7 year old	6			
	60			
Kidding rate: 40% does x 1.45 = 35 kids/year (Reproduction rate 1.45)				
Kid does		Death rate 30%		
	18	- 5 deaths		
		- 13 doe weaners		
Doe weaners		Death rate 30%		
	13	- 4 deaths		
		- 9 doe recruits		
Kid billies		Death rate 30%		
	18	- 5 deaths		
		- 2 billy recruits		
		- 11 wether recruits		
Wether weaners				
Weaners	11	+ 11 recruits		
2 year old	8	- 3 deaths (30%)		
3 year old	4	- 4 deaths (25%)		
	23	- 4 slaughtered @ 30 kg	120	kg LW
Billy weaners		Death rate 25%		
Weaners	2	+ 2 recruits		
2 year old	1	- 1 death		
3 year old	1	- 1 slaughtered @ 40 kg	40	kg LW
	4			
Total meat output			160	kg LW
			or 83.2	kg DW
Production per TLU		7.63 kg meat DW		

Total TLU = 10.2 (Table 5.7)

Note: This flock cannot maintain itself and would be dependent on occasional flush seasons to rebuild numbers or intake from outside.

TABLE A6.19
Herd performance calculations for the goat pastoral system (nomadic distant) at high inputs

Base herd structure		Transfers	Output	
Does		Death rate 15%		
2 year old	12	+ 12 recruits		
3 year old	10	- 8 deaths		
4 year old	10	- 4 culls @ 28 kg LW	112	kg LW
5 year old	8			
6 year old	8			
7 year old	6			
	54			
Kidding rate: 60% does x 1.45 = 47 kids/year				
(Reproduction rate 1.45)				
Kid does		Death rate 25%		
	24	- 6 deaths		
		- 18 doe weaners		
Doe weaners		Death rate 30%		
	18	- 6 deaths		
		- 12 doe recruits		
Kid billies		Death rate 25%		
	23	- 6 deaths		
		- 2 billy recruits		
		- 15 wether recruits		
Wether weaners				
Weaners	15	+ 15 recruits		
2 year old	10	- 5 deaths (30%)		
3 year old	8	- 2 deaths (25%)		
	33	- 8 slaughtered @ 40 kg	320	kg LW
Billy weaners		Death rate 25%		
Weaners	2	+ 2 recruits		
2 year old	1	- 1 death		
3 year old	1	- 1 slaughtered @ 45 kg	45	kg LW
	4			
Total meat output			477	kg LW
			or 245	kg DW
Production per TLU		19.8 kg meat DW		

Total TLU = 12.5 (Table 5.7)

TABLE A6.20
Herd performance parameters for the sheep pastoral systems

Parameters	Semi-nomadic	Nomadic distant
Female breeder mortality rate	0.10	0.15
Male breeder mortality rate	0.25	0.25
Female replacement mortality rate	0.25	0.25
Male replacement mortality rate	0.25	0.25
Young mortality rate	0.10	0.20
Fertility rate	0.65	0.50
Prolificacy rate	1.25	1.25
Breeder females per male	12.5	12.5
Female breeder carcase weight (tonnes)	0.028	0.025
Male breeder carcase weight (tonnes)	0.035	0.030
Slaughter stock carcase weight (tonnes)	0.035	0.030
Milk yield per lactation (tonnes)	0	0
Fraction of females milked	0	0

TABLE A6.21
Herd performance calculations for the sheep pastoral system (nomadic distant) at low inputs

Base herd structure		Transfers	Output	
Ewes		Death rate 15%		
2 year old	11	+ 12 recruits		
3 year old	11	- 12 deaths		
4 year old	10			
5 year old	9			
6 year old	9			
	50			
Lambing rate: 50% does x 1.25 = 31 lambs/year (Reproduction rate 1.25)				
Ewe lambs		Death rate 20%		
	16	- 3 deaths		
		- 13 ewe recruits		
Ewe weaners		Death rate 25%		
	13	- 4 deaths		
		- 11 ewe recruits		
Ram lambs		Death rate 20%		
	15	- 3 deaths		
		- 2 ram recruits		
		- 10 wether recruits		
Wethers				
Weaners	10	+ 10 recruits		
2 year old	8	- 2 deaths (25%)		
3 year old	6	- 2 deaths (15%)		
	24	- 6 slaughtered @ 30 kg LW	180	kg LW
Rams		Death rate 25%		
Weaners	2	+ 2 recruits		
2 year old	1	- 1 death		
3 year old	1	- 1 slaughtered @ 30 kg	30	kg LW
	4			
Total meat output			210	kg LW
			or 109	kg DW
Production per TLU		8.95 kg meat DW		

Total TLU = 12.2 (Table 5.7)

Note: This flock is barely self-sustaining.

TABLE A6.22
Herd performance calculations for the sheep pastoral system (semi-nomadic) at high inputs

Base herd structure		Transfers	Output	
Ewes		Death rate 10%		
2 year old	11	+ 11 recruits		
3 year old	11	- 5 deaths		
4 year old	10	- 6 culls @ 28 kg LW	168	kg LW
5 year old	9			
6 year old	9			
	50			
Lambing rate: 65% does x 1.25 = 31 lambs/year				
(Reproduction rate 1.25)				
Ewe lambs		Death rate 10%		
	20	- 2 deaths		
	9	- 18 ewe recruits		
Ewe weaners		Death rate 25%		
	18	- 6 deaths		
		- 11 ewe recruits		
		- 1 cull @ 15 kg LW	15	kg LW
Ram lambs		Death rate 10%		
	20	- 2 deaths		
		- 2 ram recruits		
		- 10 wether recruits		
		- 6 culls @ 8 kg LW	48	kg LW
Wethers				
Weaners	10	+ 10 recruits		
2 year old	5	- 2/3 deaths (25%)		
3 year old	5	- 1 death (10%)		
	20	6/7 slaughtered @ 35 kg LW	227.5	kg LW
Rams		Death rate 25%		
Weaners	2	+ 2 recruits		
2 year old	1	- 1 death		
3 year old	1	- 1 slaughtered @ 35 kg	35	kg LW
	4			
Total meat output			493.5	kg LW
			or 256.6	kg DW
Production per TLU		19.4 kg meat DW		

Total TLU = 13.2 (Table 5.7)

TABLE A6.23
Herd performance parameters for the camel pastoral systems (nomadic)

Parameters	Nomadic
Fertility rate	0.5
Prolificacy rate	1
Bulls per cow	0.14
Milk yield per lactation in tonnes	0.6
Fraction of females milked	0.5
Cow mortality rate	0.1
Bull mortality rate	0.17
Female replacement mortality rate	0.09
Male replacement mortality rate	0.08
Female young mortality rate	0.5
Male young mortality rate	0.5
Other stock mortality rate	0.83
Female breeder carcase weight (tonnes)	0.35
Male breeded carcase weight (tonnes)	0.40
Carcase weight of other stock (tonnes)	0.40
Presence of males in the system	yes

TABLE A6.24

Herd performance calculations for the camel pastoral system (nomadic) at low inputs

Base herd structure		Transfers	Output	
Breeding cows[1]		Death rate 10%		
6 year old	5	+ 4 recruits		
7 year old	5			
8 year old	5			
9 year old	5	- 4 deaths		
10 year old	4			
11 year old	4			
12 year old	4			
13 year old	4			
14 year old	3			
15 year old	<u>3</u>			
	42			
Calves under 1 year		50% calving rate		
Heifers	11	Death rate 50%		
Net live	6	- 5 deaths		
calves		- 6 recruits to replacement herd		
Replacement females		Death rate 9%		
1 year old	6	+ 6 recruits		
2 year old	5	- 2 deaths		
3 year old	4	- 4 recruits to cow herd		
4 year old	4			
5 year old	<u>4</u>			
	22			
Bull calves		Death rate 50%		
Bull calves	10	- 5 deaths		
Net live		- 4 to growing bulls		
calves		- 1 slaughtered @ 100 kg	100	kg LW
Growing bulls		Death rate 8%		
1 year old	4	+ 4 recruits		
2 year old	3	- 1 death		
3 year old	3	- 1 bull recruit		
4 year old	<u>3</u>	- 2 castrate recruits		
	13			
Bulls		Death rate 17%		
5 year old	1	+ 1 recruit		
6 year old	1	- 1 death		
7 year old	1			
8 year old	1			
9 year old	1			
10 year old	<u>1</u>			
	6			

TABLE A.24 Continued

Base herd structure		Transfers	Output	
Castrates				
5 year old	2	+ 2 recruits		
6 year old	2	- 1 death		
7 year old	2	- 1 slaughtered @ 400 kg	400	kg LW
8 year old	2			
9 year old	1			
10 year old	1			
11 year old	1			
12 year old	1			
	12			
Total meat output			500	kg LW
			or 250	kg DW
Total milk output (21 cows x 600 litres)			12 600 litres	
		Milk	Meat	
Production per TLU		96.2 litres	1.9 kg DW	

Total TLU = 131 (Table 5.8)

[1]　Herd size can only be maintained by holding all old cows

WORLD SOIL RESOURCES REPORTS

1. Report of the First Meeting of the Advisory Panel on the Soil Map of the World, Rome, 19-23 June 1961.**
2. Report of the First Meeting on Soil Survey, Correlation and Interpretation for Latin America, Rio de Janeiro, Brazil, 28-31 May 1962**
3. Report of the First Soil Correlation Seminar for Europe, Moscow, USSR, 16-28 July 1962.**
4. Report of the First Soil Correlation Seminar for South and Central Asia, Tashkent, Uzbekistan, USSR, 14 September-2 October 1962.**
5. Report of the Fourth Session of the Working Party on Soil Classification and Survey (Subcommission on Land and Water Use of the European Commission on Agriculture), Lisbon, Portugal, 6-10 March 1963.**
6. Report of the Second Meeting of the Advisory Panel on the Soil Map of the World, Rome, 9-11 July 1963.**
7. Report of the Second Soil Correlation Seminar for Europe, Bucharest, Romania, 29 July-6 August 1963.**
8. Report of the Third Meeting of the Advisory Panel on the Soil Map of the World, Paris, 3 January 1964.**
9. Adequacy of Soil Studies in Paraguay, Bolivia and Peru, November-December 1963.**
10. Report on the Soils of Bolivia, January 1964.**
11. Report on the Soils of Paraguay, January 1964.**
12. Preliminary Definition, Legend and Correlation Table for the Soil Map of the World, Rome, August 1964.**
13. Report of the Fourth Meeting of the Advisory Panel on the Soil Map of the World, Rome, 16-21 May 1964.**
14. Report of the Meeting on the Classification and Correlation of Soils from Volcanic Ash, Tokyo, Japan, 11-27 June 1964.**
15. Report of the First Session of the Working Party on Soil Classification, Survey and Soil Resources of the European Commission on Agriculture, Florence, Italy, 1-3 October 1964.**
16. Detailed Legend for the Third Draft on the Soil Map of South America, June 1965.**
17. Report of the First Meeting on Soil Correlation for North America, Mexico, 1-8 February 1965.**
18. The Soil Resources of Latin America, October 1965.**
19. Report of the Third Correlation Seminar for Europe: Bulgaria, Greece, Romania, Turkey, Yugoslavia, 29 August-22 September 1965.**
20. Report of the Meeting of Rapporteurs, Soil Map of Europe (Scale 1:1 000 000) (Working Party on Soil Classification and Survey of the European Commission on Agriculture), Bonn, Federal Republic of Germany, 29 November-3 December 1965.**
21. Report of the Second Meeting on Soil Survey, Correlation and Interpretation for Latin America, Rio de Janeiro, Brazil, 13-16 July 1965.**
22. Report of the Soil Resources Expedition in Western and Central Brazil, 24 June-9 July 1965.**
23. Bibliography on Soils and Related Sciences for Latin America (1st edition), December 1965.**
24. Report on the Soils of Paraguay (2nd edition), August 1964.**
25. Report of the Soil Correlation Study Tour in Uruguay, Brazil and Argentina, June-August 1964.**
26. Report of the Meeting on Soil Correlation and Soil Resources Appraisal in India, New Delhi, India, 5-15 April 1965.**
27. Report of the Sixth Session of the Working Party on Soil Classification and Survey of the European Commission on Agriculture, Montpellier, France, 7-11 March 1967.**
28. Report of the Second Meeting on Soil Correlation for North America, Winnipeg-Vancouver, Canada, 25 July-5 August 1966.**
29. Report of the Fifth Meeting of the Advisory Panel on the Soil Map of the World, Moscow, USSR, 20-28 August 1966.**
30. Report of the Meeting of the Soil Correlation Committee for South America, Buenos Aires, Argentina, 12-19 December 1966.**
31. Trace Element Problems in Relation to Soil Units in Europe (Working Party on Soil Classification and Survey of the European Commission on Agriculture), Rome, 1967.**
32. Approaches to Soil Classification, 1968.**
33. Definitions of Soil Units for the Soil Map of the World, April 1968.**
34. Soil Map of South America 1:5 000 000, Draft Explanatory Text, November 1968.**
35. Report of a Soil Correlation Study Tour in Sweden and Poland, 27 September-14 October 1968.**
36. Meeting of Rapporteurs, Soil Map of Europe (Scale 1:1 000 000) (Working Party on Soil Classification and Survey of the European Commission on Agriculture), Poitiers, France 21-23 June 1967.**
37. Supplement to Definition of Soil Units for the Soil Map of the World, July 1969.**
38. Seventh Session of the Working Party on Soil Classification and Survey of the European Commission on Agriculture, Varna, Bulgaria, 11-13 September 1969.**
39. A Correlation Study of Red and Yellow Soils in Areas with a Mediterranean Climate.**
40. Report of the Regional Seminar of the Evaluation of Soil Resources in West Africa, Kumasi, Ghana, 14-19 December 1970.**
41. Soil Survey and Soil Fertility Research in Asia and the Far East, New Delhi, 15-20 February 1971.**
42. Report of the Eighth Session of the Working Party on Soil Classification and Survey of the European Commission on Agriculture, Helsinki, Finland, 5-7 July 1971.**

43.   Report of the Ninth Session of the Working Party on Soil Classification and Survey of the European Commission on Agriculture, Ghent, Belgium 28-31 August 1973.**

44.   First Meeting of the West African Sub-Committee on Soil Correlation for Soil Evaluation and Management, Accra, Ghana, 12-19 June 1972.**

45.   Report of the Ad Hoc Expert Consultation on Land Evaluation, Rome, Italy, 6-8 January 1975.**

46.   First Meeting of the Eastern African Sub-Committee for Soil Correlation and Land Evaluation, Nairobi, Kenya, 11-16 March 1974.**

47.   Second Meeting of the Eastern African Sub-Committee for Soil Correlation and Land Evaluation, Addis Ababa, Ethiopia, 25-30 October 1976.

48.   Report on the Agro-Ecological Zones Project, Vol. 1 - Methodology and Results for Africa, 1978. Vol. 2 - Results for Southwest Asia, 1978.

49.   Report of an Expert Consultation on Land Evaluation Standards for Rainfed Agriculture, Rome, Italy, 25-28 October 1977.

50.   Report of an Expert Consultation on Land Evaluation Criteria for Irrigation, Rome, Italy, 27 February-2 March 1979.

51.   Third Meeting of the Eastern African Sub-Committee for Soil Correlation and Land Evaluation, Lusaka, Zambia, 18-30 April 1978.

52.   Land Evaluation Guidelines for Rainfed Agriculture, Report of an Expert Consultation, 12-14 December 1979.

53.   Fourth Meeting of the West African Sub-Committee for Soil Correlation and Land Evaluation, Banjul, The Gambia, 20-27 October 1979.

54.   Fourth Meeting of the Eastern African Sub-Committee for Soil Correlation and Land Evaluation, Arusha, Tanzania, 27 October-4 November 1980.

55.   Cinquième réunion du Sous-Comité Ouest et Centre africain de corrélation des sols pour la mise en valeur des terres, Lomé, Togo, 7-12 décembre 1981.

56.   Fifth Meeting of the Eastern African Sub-Committee for Soil Correlation and Land Evaluation, Wad Medani, Sudan, 5-10 December 1983.

57.   Sixième réunion du Sous-Comité Ouest et Centre Africain de corrélation des sols pour la mise en valeur des terres, Niamey, Niger, 6-12 février 1984.

58.   Sixth Meeting of the Eastern African Sub-Committee for Soil Correlation and Land Evaluation, Maseru, Lesotho, 9-18 October 1985.

59.   Septième réunion du Sous-Comité Ouest et Centre africain de corrélation des sols pour la mise en valeur des terres, Ouagadougou, Burkina Faso, 10-17 novembre 1985.

60.   Revised Legend, Soil Map of the World, FAO-Unesco-ISRIC, 1988. Reprinted 1990.

61.   Huitième réunion du Sous-Comité Ouest et Centre africain de corrélation des sols pour la mise en valeur des terres, Yaoundé, Cameroun, 19-28 janvier 1987.

62.   Seventh Meeting of the East and Southern African Sub-Committee for Soil Correlation and Evaluation, Gaborone, Botswana, 30 March-8 April 1987.

63.   Neuvième réunion du Sous-Comité Ouest et Centre africain de corrélation des sols pour la mise en valeur des terres, Cotonou, Bénin, 14-23 novembre 1988.

64.   FAO-ISRIC Soil Database (SDB), 1989.

65.   Eighth Meeting of the East and Southern African Sub-Committee for Soil Correlation and Land Evaluation, Harare, Zimbabwe, 9-13 October 1989.

66.   World soil resources. An explanatory note on the FAO World Soil Resources Map at 1:25 000 000 scale, 1991.

67.   Digitized Soil Map of the World, Volume 1: Africa, Release 1.0, November 1991. Volume 2: North and Central America. Volume 3: Central and South America. Volume 4: Europe and West of the Urals. Volume 5: North East Asia. Volume 6: Near East and Far East. Volume 7: South East Asia and Oceania.

68.   Land Use Planning Applications. Proceedings of the FAO Expert Consultation 1990, Rome, 10-14 December 1990.

69.   Dixième réunion du Sous-Comité Ouest et Centre africain de corrélation des sols pour la mise en valeur des terres, Bouaké, Odienné, Côte d'Ivoire, Côte d'Ivoire, 5-12 november 1990.

70.   Ninth Meeting of the East and Southern African Sub-Committee for Soil Correlation and Land Evaluation, Lilongwe, Malawi, 25 November - 2 December 1991.

71.   Agro-ecological land resources assessment for agricultural development planning. A case study of Kenya. Resources data base and land productivity. Main Report. Technical Annex 1: Land resources. Technical Annex 2: Soil erosion and productivity. Technical Annex 3: Agro-climatic and agro-edaphic suitabilities for barley, oat, cowpea, green gram and pigeonpea. Technical Annex 4: Crop productivity. Technical Annex 5: Livestock productivity. Technical Annex 6: Fuelwood productivity. Technical Annex 7: Systems documentation guide to computer programs for land productivity assessments. Technical Annex 8: Crop productivity assessment: results at district level. 1991.

**   Out of print